Life Without the Father

Life Without the Father
A MAN'S GUIDE TO FATHERHOOD

DR. CLYDE A. STEWART

TATE PUBLISHING & Enterprises

Published by Tate Publishing & Enterprises, LLC
127 E. Trade Center Terrace | Mustang, Oklahoma 73064 USA
1.888.361.9473 | www.tatepublishing.com

Tate Publishing is committed to excellence in the publishing industry. The company reflects the philosophy established by the founders, based on Psalm 68:11,
"The Lord gave the word and great was the company of those who published it."

Book design copyright © 2009 by Tate Publishing, LLC. All rights reserved.
Cover design by Tyler Evans
Interior design by Joey Garrett

Published in the United States of America

ISBN: 978-1-61566-222-7
Family & Relationships / Parenting / Fatherhood
09.11.02

And you fathers, do not provoke your children to wrath, but bring them up in the training and admonition of the Lord.

Ephesians 6:4, NKJV

Acknowledgment

To my dear wife, Florence, whom I affectionately call "Flo-Flo"; you are the earthly force in my life that keeps me grounded. You inspire me to follow my dreams. You are the support system that no one else knows about except the Father. Flo, you have blessed me with two beautiful children who have your strength and honesty. You have been by my side for thirty-five years now, and for that I am deeply grateful to God. If no one else believed in me and thought I would not complete my assignment, you did. God knows all things, and he knew I could not be me without you. Truly, I would not be the man of God I am today without your influence.

To my children, Anthony and Charmaine; I thank God for the reflection you have been of my desire to make the world a better place by bringing children up in the fear and admonition of the Lord.

To my mother Merle, who faithfully raised six children and taught me the meaning of hard work and dedication.

To my eldest sister Linda, who acted as our surrogate mother while mama worked two jobs.

To my youngest sister Charlotte for her encouragement and support.

To my spiritual father, Apostle Frederick K.C. Price, who was the first example I had of a father; I thank God daily for you.

Special thanks to my administrative assistant, Desiree, for her countless hours typing and editing the manuscript.

And to all the members of Westside Christian Center and friends in ministry, thank you for your love, prayers, and support.

Table of Contents

Introduction

This book is written as a guide for successful fatherhood. It contains spiritual and natural insights that will help men fulfill their responsibilities as fathers. If a man takes God's perspective on the importance of being a father, knowing he will be the deciding factor in fulfilling a child's destiny, I believe men will view their role in a more serious light. This book is in no way written to diminish the role and need of mothers. Nor is it written with the suggestion that grandparents, teachers, stepparents, or society have no role in the development of a child. However, the role of a father is the foundation of a child's stability, both spiritually and emotionally. There is no other person in a child's life who can build the necessary strength that a child needs to be successful. A father is the one person responsible for a child's existence in the earth. The Word of God tells us, "as long as the earth remains, there will be seed, time, and harvest."

Before there can be a birth (harvest), there must be a seed. And, men—you are the only one to whom God has entrusted the seed of life. Thus, you are responsible to produce an environment that your seed can grow, develop properly, and bear fruit that will bring glory and honor to the Heavenly Father. If you are not born again, you will not get the spiritual impact intended for you. This book is written with the help of the Holy Spirit and the Word of God, both of which are spiritual supernatural forces. The focus target group for this book is Christian men, men who are fathers, men who hope to become fathers, and for any man who have experienced life without a father. I believe it will help you in receiving your healing from the experience of missing your escort through life.

> Children's children are the crown of old men, And the glory of children is their father.
>
> Proverbs 17:6, NKJV

> Fathers, do not provoke your children, lest they become discouraged.
>
> Colossians 3:21, ESV

What is a Father?

I want to start by defining "father." The definition will come by way of accepted definitions in our society, as well as life experiences. Giving a biblical explanation of what a father is will help us understand what a father does. According to Vine's Complete Expository Dictionary of Old and New Testament Words, the Latin word for "father" is *pater*. Pater is defined in the Bible as a nourisher (you would think this was a mother's role); a strength-giver; a satisfier; one who supplies needs: spiritual, emotional, and physical.

Before a man becomes a father, he should first be mature spiritually, emotionally, and financially. I do not mean he should be perfect, rich, or a Bible scholar. However, he should be prepared to escort a child through life based on the Word of God. I have found the only way to become an escort is for a man to be born-again with a godly plan for his child before the child arrives on planet

Earth. A father is a man of responsibility. When a man takes on the job of a father, he is announcing to the world he can handle responsibility.

Let's take a look at the best role model in the universe of a father. God the Father created man and required of *himself* to be responsible for the needs of man. God's first response to the needs of man was to provide a safe, suitable place where his children could grow, be nourished, and be provided for. According to the Bible, God created the heavens and the earth. Based on Genesis 1:1–2 (NKJV), "The earth was without form and void; and darkness was on the face of the deep."

The Hebrew account of Genesis 1:1–2 is there was chaos on the earth. The earth in this condition was not a healthy place for a father to bring up his responsibilities (children).

Man of God, if there is chaos in your life, either spiritually, emotionally, or financially, you are not prepared to become a father. I have found if there is a void or chaos in one or more of these areas in your life, you will not be the effective escort God called you to be. Now remember, I'm dealing with this topic from God's perspective. God always sets the standard at a "ten." We are to press toward the mark of God's best; not the world's standard, and not what we may have learned from ungodly relatives, or society. Based on today's standards, a father's role may be performed by women, the government, grandparents, or males commonly referred to as "babies' daddies." None of these people, and others not mentioned, fall under the definition of a father. Remember, a father is a man who is accountable for keeping a spiritually healthy, physically and emotionally safe place, void of chaos and darkness in his responsibility's (child's) life. When God saw the condition of the planet in which his children were to come, he got the place in order so that it could meet the needs of his children.

God Set the Home in Order

Before God brought man onto the scene, he told the earth to bring forth light. He put the days in order so as to provide stability in the life of his children.

> God called the light day and the darkness, He called night. So the evening and the morning were the first day.
>
> Genesis 1:5, NKJV

Children need to have order in their lives so they can grow and become stable, productive adults.

When children know what to expect at home and the expectation is order, peace, and love, children feel safe and cared for. God the Father knew this, so his example was to show us order in his creation. Men, when you bring your seed into the earth, your life should have godly order in it, along with natural order.

God the Father should be your standard as to how you care for your seed. Can you imagine if we did not have an expectation of morning or night? Suppose we did not have an expectation of winter, spring, summer, or fall? God said while the earth remains we can expect cold and heat, winter and summer; day and night shall not cease (Genesis 8:26). What I have just described is order. God did not want his children to get up one day to freezing temperatures and one hundred degrees heat the next day. He knew we could plan our lives and have more stability, knowing the sun would rise and set again, right on schedule. God is a Father of order, and men should take that principle and use it in bringing up their children. I recall the time when my son was a little fellow. He had a time to go to bed, a time to rise (on school days), a time for play, and a time for homework. I loved to get him up in the morning, help get his breakfast, and see him off to school. I believe this set the tone for a safe, stable day at school. If something went wrong at school, Anthony knew things would be safe and in order at home. Children want and need to know, 'When I get home, daddy will be there; daddy keeps me safe; daddy will talk to me; daddy will play with me; daddy will be there for me." Have you noticed how many times God told the children of Israel, *"I will never leave you nor forsake you"*? God took the children of Israel as his own and made a covenant with them, "I'm here for you. In all times, your good days and your bad days, I cannot leave you nor forsake you."

Our children need to know daddy planned for their arrival into the earth realm, and that he made a vow to never leave them nor forsake them, to be there for them, and to escort them through life.

Your Connection to Your Seed

When God had the earth in order to receive his seed, he said,

> Let us make man in our image according to our likeness, and let them have dominion.
>
> Genesis 1:26, NKJV

The Bible goes on to tell us God created man in his own image—in the image of God, he created mankind (Genesis 1:26–27). God created *male* mankind and *female* mankind—not one superior over the other, but different. Men and women have different functions and roles. Men cannot be mothers, and women cannot be fathers. We learn that God said we were in his image and in his likeness. Mankind is a spirit first; if we read the Bible correctly the Bible says God is a spirit (John 4:24). So since God is a spirit, and he made us in his image and in his likeness, we have a connection to the Father that draws all men unto him. Mankind cannot keep himself from the questions, "Where did I come from? Why am I here?" This need to know the Father is birthed into us—the spirit part of us. And we all have an awareness that there is a God. When a man brings a child into the earth realm, the child has a built-in connection that wants to know, "Where did I come from? I need to know my father." When children do not know the answer to that built-in question because of a physical or psychological disconnection, they are left with a void, and chaos will sooner or later become part of their lives. Why? Because they have been disconnected from the father. Men, when you release your seed into the earth realm, it is forever connected to you, and your children will never become the whole person they could have been, given the chance to stay connected to you. I'm not suggesting that people who have been disconnected from their fathers will *never* be able to be completely functional.

I myself was a child disconnected from my father at the age of eight. It took the power of God and becoming born again to get me to where God had intended for me to be. However, there were thirty years of chaos, searching, and hurting that I went through. This period of being "lost in the wilderness" was not God's best. God put us in the loins of our fathers, so that his will could be done on earth. When a man is not mature enough to cultivate his seed, the seed and the earth will suffer. You may know of others who have been disconnected from their fathers, and they may seem to be happy, healthy, productive adults with families of their own. What you may not know is the pain and chaos they endured because of a life without the father. This book was not written out of anger or bitterness, or to bash men who have not lived up to their responsibilities. It was written to bring healing and definition to children who are in chaos as a result of being disconnected from the father. There are millions of people confused and unfulfilled who have not realized the cause for their discontentment. If you are a person who was disconnected, there are what I call "emotional leaks" in your life.

The first step to fixing the leak is to find out where the crack is. Emotional leaks manifest themselves in depression, anger, wrath, bitterness, and feelings of unfulfillment that can be the result of a disconnection.

This book is targeted for the believer who may have experienced life without the father. Without Jesus, no therapy on earth can help you with this disconnection. Once you were born again, you were put in position for wholeness and soundness, with nothing missing and nothing broken for your life. It is a tragedy that people become born again and do not experience the whole life God the Father gave them through the blood of Jesus.

When you received Jesus, your spirit changed instantly. That's the good news. The other side of the coin is that our bodies and our minds did not change instantly. That is why the Bible tells us in 1 Thessalonians 5:23, that God himself *"sanctifies us completely, spirit, soul and body."* God the Father wants his children to be whole spiritually, emotionally, and physically. Part of his plan was for a man, "father," to escort us through the life process. Further proof that we are a "work in progress" is that God tells us in Romans 12:12 to "present our bodies to him a living sacrifice and not to be like the world's system, but to be transformed by the renewing of our mind." The mind is the arena that contains our wills, feelings, and emotions. If the soulish (mind) part of our makeup is injured as the result of a disconnection, it will hinder our godly destiny. The fact that you are born again takes care of your eternal life, but you will have to face your natural issues in order to be the success God intended for you to be.

Fathers help children fulfill their destinies. Let's take a look at some great examples of people who found their reasons for being on earth at an appointed time.

Moses was a victim of being disconnected from the father. In Exodus 1:15, the King of Egypt commanded the Hebrew midwives to kill any male child that was born, but if the child was a girl, then she could live. See, Pharaoh knew that without any Hebrew seed in the earth realm, he would not have to fear the people's potential to overcome the affliction he was causing them. But thank God for the women in the church! The Bible says the midwives feared God and did not do as the King of Egypt commanded. They saved the male children and kept them alive (Exodus 1:17). So, because of the midwives' reverence for God, Moses came into the earth to fulfill his destiny.

As a result of Egyptian bondage, Moses' mother hid him for three months. When this was no longer feasible, she put him in a basket and sailed him downriver to be raised in what seemed to be a safer environment. However, as a result of the times, Moses became disconnected from his father. Moses' father did not divorce his mother or desert the family, but the fact is that Moses was raised as the son of Pharaoh's daughter. She named him. Moses grew up bitter and angry about the condition of his life and the lives of his brethren. Moses, like so many young men, grew up with a negative attitude, and he would take his emotional pain out in some way on somebody.

One day Moses saw an Egyptian beating a Hebrew. He looked around to see if anyone was watching, and Moses killed the Egyptian.

Pharaoh heard of the crime and issued a death warrant for Moses. Moses left town as a fugitive. He was on the Egyptian nightly news; he was on the Egyptian FBI's "Ten Most Wanted" list. Moses' emotional leaks caused him to commit murder. It reminds me of so many hurting young boys in our inner cities, killing one another, and causing pain and heartache on others because they are experiencing life without an escort. I pray this does not sound like a cop-out or an excuse for gang violence; it is simply the result of life without a father. Now, like many of us, Moses eventually married and became a father. Yet, he still had a negative picture of himself as a result of being disconnected from the father. It took divine intervention from God in order for Moses to see the greatness that was in him all along.

Men, you have some greatness that was in you all the time. It will take a connection with the Father to bring it out. Moses had some things together: he had a job and he was financially sound, if not emotionally. The Bible records in Exodus 3:1–3 that while Moses was at work one day, an angel of the Lord appeared to him in a flame of fire from the midst of a bush, and the bush was not consumed! This was a supernatural act of God, akin to us being born again.

But quite often it takes some personal ministry from God to get us over the trauma of being disconnected from living without a father. You would think after an encounter like Moses just experienced, he was ripe and ready to fulfill his assignment. Spiritually speaking, Moses was ready to go, but Moses could not accept his worth as God saw it because of his emotional state. In Exodus 3:10 God told Moses,

> …I will send you to Pharaoh that you may bring
> My people, the children of Israel, out of Egypt.
>
> Exodus 3:10, NKJV

Moses replies in the next verse (paraphrase),

> …Who am I that I should go to Pharaoh and
> that I should do something great like bring people
> out of bondage?
>
> Exodus 3:11

God quite often uses people who are in bondage to help others get free from their affliction. How many times has God spoken to our hearts to do great things with him, but because of our lack of strength or because of our disconnected escort, we would not believe that we were worthy to be used by God? God went to work on Moses' emotional leaks. Good escorts will minister to the emotional leaks that may spring up in their children from time to time. I do not want to give the impression that if a child has a "father," he will not face challenges in life. What I am suggesting is, with a life escort, he will be able to deal with and overcome the issues of life in less time and effort than a child without an escort. God immediately dealt with Moses' abandonment issues: "I will be with you. Moses, I won't abandon you. You are connected to me."

God instructed Moses to tell the children of Israel, the God of their Father Abraham, Isaac, and the God of Jacob has sent me. Because of the many years of slavery the children of Israel had endured, God had Moses tell the people, "I will move on your behalf, based on your connection with your fathers of past generations." God let the children of Israel know, "Not only am I going to take care of your spiritual needs, I will take care of your physical and emotional needs as well." Let me paraphrase what God said to Moses in Exodus 3:17, "Tell my children, I will bring them up out of their affliction and emotional leaks of depression, discouragement, and fear.

God went on to say he had a place prepared for them; a land flowing with milk and honey. God the Father knew the pain and hurt the children of Israel had endured. When people, as a whole, are disconnected from their seed, there are many obstacles to overcome. God was personally escorting Moses to his destiny. Paraphrasing what God told Moses,

> I will send you to the most powerful man on earth, but when you go, you shall not go empty-handed.
>
> Exodus 3:21

A father who is a life escort makes sure his children are equipped to handle life's challenges.

Moses, being a man who was disconnected from his father, had all sorts of self-esteem issues. Now, here he is receiving face-to-face instructions from the Most High God and all Moses could do was count his inadequacies. Moses says,

> But suppose they will not believe me or listen to my voice...?
>
> Exodus 4:1, NKJV

It is plain to see why many believers today cannot take God at his word. Because of a man, a father, who did not keep his word to them and escort them through the obstacles of life, they find it difficult to trust God the Father. We find in the book of Exodus, chapter four, verses 2–9, God the Father building confidence and trust in his son, Moses. God is spending quality time with Moses, encouraging him that he is worthy of greatness, and, with his father's help, he could pull off this awesome feat.

As a pastor, it is quite sad to see adult children of God called to greatness by God, but, because of the emotional baggage they have gathered over the years, they find it difficult to believe that God wants to use them. Now God shows Moses the things he could accomplish if he were to take God at his word. God used Moses' rod and turned it into a serpent. Poor Moses ran! God said, "Come on son, reach out your hand and take it by the tail." Moses reached out his hand, caught it, and it became a rod in his hand again. Now, after God had demonstrated Moses' potential by staying connected to him, God then recited Moses' connections to the other men in his heritage. God said,

> The people will believe I have sent you if you remind them how faithful I was to their fathers, Abraham, Isaac and Jacob.
>
> Exodus 4:5

After this, you would think Moses was ready to step out and fulfill his calling. But no, like so many others who have been disconnected from their fathers, Moses was still without self-esteem. Moses tells God,

> I do not know how to communicate effectively and I also have a speech impediment.
>
> Exodus 4:10

Often, when children have not experienced the proper love and commitment from their fathers, there are emotional scars that will manifest in a physical way. There are many children in the school system today who have been diagnosed with some sort of learning disability. When we look into the backgrounds of these children, more often than not, they are being reared without a father.

Throughout my professional career as a correctional counselor, I have seen hundreds of cases of individuals below the grade levels, with ninety-five percent of those cases being children without fathers. Now, a good father will stick with his children even though they are not progressing in an endeavor. God did not give up on Moses. Fathers, do not give up on your children. It does not matter what their age is; they need your wisdom and love. Moses is approximately ninety years old at this time, but he still needed encouragement from the Father. Many times the people of God have experienced emotional or physical trauma from a life with the father. The results of this disconnection in childhood will often hinder the God-given talent placed in them at birth.

As a pastor, I see potential in the people of God. However, I don't always see it developed and used. In counseling session after counseling session, I find the believer who is struggling with his or her fulfillment had experienced life without a father. This was the case with Moses, and God in his wisdom called Moses' brother, Aaron, to support him. Now Moses had the gift of leadership, but his self-esteem was attacked, so he focused on his lack of ability to communicate effectively. Aaron was not leadership material, but he was an effective communicator. God pulled Moses' confidence up by telling him his brother, Aaron who is "good with words, I know he is." (Exodus 4:14, Message Remix), would go with Moses. Children need their fathers to help evaluate and identify their strong points and areas that need developing. Without this fatherly insight from God, Moses would not have had the courage to step out into his destiny. How many men and women have been afraid to step out into their destiny because they did not have a father to escort them? I personally have struggled with the writing of this God-inspired book. I will share later about overcoming fear to step into my destiny. I experienced life without a father and, at times, I have to remind myself, "Jesus gave you a new life; you have been born again and God the Father has healed you from all emotional leaks. Pursue your destiny." Our flesh and our minds will try to relive and rethink the shortcomings of our natural lives. We are to remind ourselves that the person who was disconnected from his natural father has a new connection with the Most High God.

Let us return to Moses and his encounter with the Father. Earlier Moses had asked God, "What should I tell the children of Israel the name of the God of their fathers is? What name should I use?" God said to Moses,

> I am who I am. Thus you shall say to the children of Israel, 'I am' has sent me to you.
>
> Exodus 3:14, NKJV

God was describing himself as the self-existent one; the eternal one who always has been and always will be; ever-present and living God. Now we as believers know there is only one God. No human can even be compared to God. But I want you, for a moment, to take a look at life through the eyes of a child when he or she looks at their father. To a child, their father is "God" as far as they are concerned. Their father always was and always will be. To an earthly child, their father is the alpha and the omega; he is omnipotent and omnipresent. A good father knows what his child is doing, where they are emotionally, and is adept at "seeing" them when they misbehave. My children thought I could hear and see through walls. Whenever they were misbehaving or had injured themselves, father was always there. Hear me, fathers; your role to a child's development is so vital that if you don't or won't fulfill your duty, you are causing your child to face a life of searching for their connection. Instead of focusing on their destiny, children need to feel safe and protected. Moses was inquiring of God if this thing was going to work; how do I know I can count on you to protect me? All of Moses' excuses and questioning were focused around his feeling safe and secure, and that there was One greater than he that he could count on. Fathers, in your children's eyes you are "God." You are greater than them. You do have their answers. You are capable of protecting them from danger, and if they know they can run home to you for help, it causes them to grow up emotionally secure.

I recall one afternoon when my son was about ten years old; he and a neighbor friend were out riding their bikes, having fun—doing what boys do. On this particular afternoon, Anthony and his friend were riding their bikes in a dirt field down the street from our home. A man sleeping in the field yelled at the boys and told them to get away from his tree. Anthony and his friend were so frightened that they ran off and left their bikes in the field. At this time I was running my own business in another city, and I was about fifteen minutes from our home. Anthony called me at my office and told me what happened. I immediately began to thank God for his angels watching over Anthony and his friend. I got in my car and drove home. Anthony and his friend were standing in the front yard waiting for me. I could see the confusion and fear in their faces. They assured me they had done nothing to provoke the man; I had them get in the car and show me where they had left their bikes. As we began to navigate the field and I escorted them to the tree line, I noticed the fear leaving Anthony. His chest poked out, "My father is here, and he will protect me and get back what belongs to me." We found the bikes; but the man was gone. I had the boys put their bikes into the trunk of the car and I escorted them back home. I am certain, to this day, that if my son had to face that situation alone and had lost his bike, it would have adversely affected his ability to feel safe and protected. The neighborhood friend, whose father did not raise him and was not available to protect him, has not made healthy choices in his adult life. He is a young man today, and as we see him from time to time, he has yet to grow up and make sound choices for his life. He is yet another child disconnected from his father.

God, who is our heavenly Father, has given us Jesus to heal our wounds and mend our broken hearts. And just like I was able to retrieve my son's bike, God can restore all that Satan has stolen from us as a result of not having a healthy connection with our earthly fathers. Once Moses was able to receive God's commitment to escort him, he was able to step out into his destiny. In Exodus 4:15, God assured Moses that he would teach him what to do. God has ordained that children learn from their fathers what they are to do to experience success in life. Just like Moses could not have been successful without instruction and equipment from God, many children must face life without proper instruction and equipment to navigate life, because of life without a father. Fathers are anointed to equip their children for the trials and tests of life. Mothers are vital and important to children as well, but a mother cannot teach what a man can, simply because she is a woman. She is not lower than or less than a man; she is not a man and cannot fulfill the role of a father. Fathers are natural defenders and protectors; just like mothers are anointed with certain abilities that display tenderness, kindness, and gentle support to her children.

Moses was in need of a firm hand so that he could have the necessary confidence to move forward. My assertion is that it takes a man to produce the seed in the earth realm, and it takes a man to cultivate the seed in order for it to reach its maximum potential and destiny. God the Father in this nurturing mode was cultivating Moses' potential by showing him, "You are important to me." Children draw strength and encouragement from their fathers when they are given these, what I like to call, "individual encounters" throughout their childhood. Moses, on Mt. Horeb, had an "individual encounter" with God, a divine visitation. Remember I stated earlier, fathers: you are like God to your children. God took time to give Moses individual instructions and direction. Fathers, you are not too busy to give your children individual encounters. It can make all the difference in the world in your child's ability to master certain tasks and build up their self-image. When Anthony was eight years old, he was in a pee-wee football league. The league consisted of boys aged seven and a half to nine years old. One evening the boys had to perform tackling drills. My son had never played football before and could not bring his opponent down. The next day I got a duffel bag and stuffed it with old blankets and towels and had an "individual encounter" with my son. I encouraged him and taught him how to hit and wrap up his opponent in order to effectively make a tackle. My son returned to practice the next week and, with all confidence and self-worth, he did not miss a single tackle during the tackling drills.

God let Moses know, "With me as your teacher, you can tackle any problem and bring down any obstacle you will ever face in life." I believe as a result of such an "individual encounter" with his father, my son has been able to tackle the issues of life without depending upon substances or allowing negative influences to weaken him from the strength that he drew from his father. I trust that you are not reading this as my blowing my own horn and saying, "Look at what a great dad I am." My intent is to share with you everyday father and child individual encounters that make an impact on children. If you are being held captive by emotional leaks because of life without the father, you can identify these barriers so as to overcome them with a prayer of deliverance from the Lord Jesus Christ.

Moses was able to face the greatest army in the land, defeat the greatest king of his time parting the Red Sea, and lead others out of captivity.

The purpose of this book is to lead the multitudes out of captivity who have been damaged as a result of life without their father. When children have a lifetime of individual encounters, they take the character of their fathers, good or bad. I have found in my experiences, "like father, like son." God told Moses,

> …Is not Aaron the Levite your brother? I know that he can speak well.
> And look, he is also coming out to meet you. When he sees you, he will be glad in his heart. .
> So he shall be your spokesman to the people. And

he himself shall be as a mouth for you, and you shall be to him as God."

Exodus 4:14, 16 NKJV

In other words, "Moses, as a direct result of being in my presence, you will take on my wisdom, my character, and my strength." This is why so many children are emotionally lost and spiritually in despair. They have no father to plug into and draw life-giving strength from. They have grown up disconnected from their father. I counsel teenaged children on a weekly basis; approximately one hundred teens in a six-month period. All one hundred teens have grown up without their fathers. All one hundred teens express they feel as though they are not whole and are not valuable; all one hundred teens are angry and distant from mainstream society; all one hundred teens will grow up and become adults in our society. What contribution will they be capable of making to our society, feeling as though they have been disconnected from the one who sowed them into the earth? Now you may know someone who grew up in such conditions as I have described and you may say, "Bill grew up without a father and he turned out okay." Well, Bill may appear to be doing okay, but do you really know what Bill has had to deal with on the inside? Do you really know the emotional leaks Bill has had to overcome, or is still overcoming? Only Bill has had to contend with his self-worth; he was the one who experienced life without the father. I am giving you the view of a loving, responsible father that I described in the beginning of this chapter. I realize a great majority of children do have "contact" with their fathers. However, if the male is not connected to his seed, or if he is just present and not participating, or present and abusive, the results will be the same to the child. He or she had a father in the home, but he still did not complete his role as a father if a lifelong bond was not developed. Seed has a need to know the origin of its root system, and fathers, you are the root system to your child. Roots provide the very life essentials a tree needs to be healthy and productive. I am stating children cannot reach their potential in an emotionally healthy state, disconnected from their father. I know as you begin to ponder this view on the role of a father in a child's life, you are assessing your relationship with your own father. It is a natural, almost instinctive, response.

"Did I receive all that I need from the one who caused me to exist in the earth?" Children desire to be exposed to the love and guidance of a father. It was placed in them by the very one who planted them, their father.

Looking back, Moses learned that God's wisdom and insights placed him in a state of sureness he had never experienced before. Moses, along with Aaron, met with the elders of the children of Israel. Aaron explained the mission; Moses demonstrated the abilities of his God, and the Bible says in Exodus 4:31, "so the people believed ... " If God had not been able to get Moses to believe that he was Moses' strength, Moses would not have been capable to show the elder's the power he had received from his God. Our children must learn to believe in their abilities and attributes that God has placed in them; but without a father to bring them out, the abilities will be delayed or destroyed because a child did not have a father to bring him up to what was pre-programmed in the seed. All seed is pre-programmed to produce after its own kind. I am not asserting our children are to be exact carbon copies of us. However, since we are the fathers, we are the developers God uses to bring out his plan for our children. Moses experienced success with the elders, but when he was confronted with the daunting task of telling Pharaoh to let the people go, Pharaoh made things harder on the people of God. Of course, Moses returned to God and has an "emotional leak,"

> Lord, why have you brought trouble on this people? Why is it you have sent me?
>
> Exodus 5:22, NKJV

Moses was telling God, "Out of all the people on the planet, you picked me for such a task as this?" Moses went on to inform God,

> Since I spoke to Pharaoh in your name, he has raised the bar on evil to this people.
>
> Exodus 5:23, NKJV

Children are facing the world with the name of their fathers; their names remind them and inform others of the person they are dealing with.

Men, if you have developed your seed properly at home, they are reminded, "I am a 'Stewart'; a 'Jones'; a 'Smith.' I have a father who escorted me through life." When God gave his name to Moses, he was telling him, "Son, you have the backing of the universe at your disposal." God replied to Moses, "I am the Lord." This statement by God details Yahweh's purpose in the book of Exodus. This section is so important that most biblical theologians believe this passage to be the heart of the Pentateuch. Here the living God explains His purpose for His people. The words, "I am the Lord" begin and conclude this section (Exodus 6: 6, 8). "Lord" stands for God's name, "Yahweh." The patriarchs had known God Almighty. It is not that they had never heard the name Yahweh, but they had not known God in an intimate way. The patriarchs knew a great deal about God and had experienced his goodness in many ways. But they had not had the revelation that was granted to Moses. Fathers, your children may know your discipline; your threats; your provision for them. However, what they really need to know is the "I Am" statement, "I will be close and loving to you always."

God told Moses about his care for his people; that it was not his will for them to struggle in life and to be strangers in Egypt. When children go through life without the father, they are in a constant state of pilgrimage and searching for their roots. As long as the children of Israel stayed disconnected from God, they wandered around and were resident aliens, without citizenship in their own country.

Children need to belong; children have a need to be accepted and approved. If a father won't accept them and approve them, I have seen hundreds of boys who have joined gangs and girls who go from relationship to relationship looking for that approval.

When Moses was finally able to allow God to close up the "cracks" in his psyche, he was ready to carry out his pre-ordained purpose. Moses led an entire people out of bondage. It was in him all the time; he was pre-programmed for greatness. Every person on the planet has an individualized role to fulfill. Without an escort, it is difficult, if not impossible, to find your way. Fathers, *you* are the escorts.

Why a Father's Role Is Vital to a Child's Fulfillment

Boys' Home Prisoner in My Own Family

"Fathers, do not provoke your children, lest they become discouraged."

Colossians 3:21, ESV

I firmly believe that without a loving father in a child's life, they will not be able to effectively fulfill their role as an individual. Every human being has a need to know why he or she is here. I believe God put that into our system, and often when there is a void of knowing about our beginning, people tend to live unfulfilled, troubled lives. God said his people are destroyed for a lack of knowledge. I believe this principal parallels with natural fathers. People tend to go through troubling stages in their lives because they were disconnected from the knowledge of their fathers. We as believers know from the dilemma in our lives when we were disconnected from God we were lost, had no hope, and were bound by the conditions of sin. When children, naturally speaking, are disconnected from their father, they cannot know the direction they are to take in life because of no escort. Life is a difficult journey to maneuver without the insight and direction of a godly influence. When we are aware of our existence, we start to make choices and allow things or people to influence us. When we are without our escort, we are like sheep without a shepherd; and in life there are a lot of wolves that can take a bite out of our futures. Let's take a look at a biblical example of a child losing the influence of his father. The young man in the account of the prodigal son is not a minor, but he needed guidance. I don't want to give the impression that children are not to grow up and start a life of their own. Nor do I want you to think that after you are married, your father is to be in your business. This would violate the Word of God, which commands,

> For this reason a man will leave his father and mother, and be united to his wife, and they will become one flesh.
>
> Genesis 2:24, NIV

Having said that, notice how God tells us that a "ten" family is a father and mother. Not a single mom, not a stepdad, not a grandmother, not an uncle; but a household is to be a father and mother. If you are reading this book and are currently raising a child outside of the "ten" standard, trust God and do your best. I'm attempting to reach those who are just starting out, those who have yet to start, and those men who can ask God to help fix a family that is about to lose its escort. Let me make one last point before we get to the prodigal son. I mentioned earlier that parents are not to be in the mix (business) of their married adult or single children, for that matter. However, having said that, I believe that adult children still need guidance from their fathers. When I become aware of a situation that my adult children may need escorting through, I allow the Holy Spirit to bring it up or, for the adult children themselves to seek out guidance from their escort. Just because your child is an adult, he or she still needs an escort from time to time. I see nothing wrong with this; I believe it says, "You did such a good job when I didn't know. Even though I may think I know what I'm doing, I have a guide, a father that I can call on."

In the mid-sixties there was a television show called "Father Knows Best." Actor Robert Young played the role of the father, a man who had his family's "best" interests at heart. He escorted his children through the confusing streams of life.

Now remember, this book is not written with the intent to put down mothers or the importance of the woman in God's plan for the family. For example in the story of the prodigal son, Jesus makes no mention of the sons' mother. He said in the book of Luke,

"A certain man had two sons."

Luke 15:11, NKJV

Now we know the man could not have had two boys without a woman. Men do not possess the equipment to birth children. But I believe this bears witness to the earlier revelation in chapter one that men bear the responsibility of escorting the children through life.

Now, obviously the boy was old enough to leave home, or a good escort would not have let the boy leave with his inheritance. He did not go to mama and ask for his portion. He had a father to go to, and he made his move. I believe the man knew his son was not ready to be on his own. However, the man understood, *my son must experience this for himself.*

As God the Father allows us to make choices, a father does not make a child's way for them. A good father puts a direction in the child and when they grow older, they will not depart from righteousness as a way of life. As you look closely at the story of the prodigal son, you will see this man was mature spiritually, emotionally, and financially. He was qualified to be a life escort. The Bible says the man's son wasted his father's resources with disobedience to what he had been taught by him.

Now, don't be so hard on the boy. How much time, energy, and resources have we wasted of the Father's when we miss the mark? Before long, the boy finds himself in a far away land, broke financially, emotionally, and spiritually, in the midst of a severe famine and he began to be in want. Things had gotten so bad for the boy he found himself working on a pig farm, eating pig food. When children become disconnected from their fathers, have not ever known their fathers, or had a bad relationship with their fathers, children can find themselves with a dirty, smelly life and in want. Something or somebody is missing in their lives.

Praise God that this boy had an escort he could return to. The father had put a connection in his son that let the boy know, *Son, I am here for you.* Just like God our Father tells us over and over again,

"… I will never leave you, nor forsake you."

Hebrews 13:5, NKJV

If you find yourself dirty in sin, repent. God says, "I am waiting for you." The man's son said, "My father has servants who are living better than this. If I don't get back to the instructions of my escort, I'll perish. I will get up and go to my father." Not to mama; not to grandma; not to Aunt Mary; but to my father's house. When children have been deprived of a father, some never find their way back to a fulfilling life. They never had a genesis.

In my professional life, prior to being called to the ministry, I worked in several California state penal institutions that housed adult males, females, and juveniles. Later, my wife and I started a community-based substance abuse program for juvenile offenders. In that program, we had over six hundred children in our care over a twelve-year period, all of which had been disconnected from their fathers. Needless to say, all were troubled, hurt, angry, and bitter. Throughout my experiences, I observed case after case of a disconnection of one degree or another, and case after case of people perishing and searching for their "father's" house. You may say, "Pastor Stewart, show me some hard facts; show me some statistics." If you will be honest, you will have to admit you see the cold hard facts every day in some form or another in our schools, communities, and, sadly, sometimes in our churches: lost, hurt, angry, and bitter "children" (adolescents to senior citizens), who are still emotionally hurt from the lack of their escort through life.

The prodigal son made his way back home; he had his story all made up. "I'll tell daddy, 'I am not worthy to be your son, put me in the category of a servant.'"

But when the man, the father, saw his son still at a great distance, the Bible says the escort (the mature man) was able to forgive his son, have mercy on his son, and resume his job as father.

This is an awesome example of how God the Father showers us with mercy although we may have sinned and gotten off-track. We always knew he was waiting for us, and he is glad when we come to our spiritual senses and come back home.

This son was able to find his way back home. He knew where home was and who would be there waiting for him. I submit to you that there are too many children who don't know where "home" is or how to get back to the father. When people are in this state, they search and search all their lives for that connection to the father.

Their strength; their nourisher; their need supplier; their satisfier is missing and they become emotionally hurt, lost, angry, and empty. Many try to fill this void with drugs, alcohol, gangs, men, women, and/or careers, but nothing seems to help. There is a disconnection that most aren't even aware of; they just know something—somebody is missing.

I mentioned earlier about case after case of adults and minors whose lives went out of control and they found themselves in the California penal system. You may think these are extreme cases, people out of the norm. Well, take a look into your own individual family connections and write down the aunts, uncles, cousins, friends, neighbors whom you know. Evaluate their relationships with their fathers; you will discover that while they may not be physically incarcerated, those who did not have an escort through life are bound up emotionally, socially, or spiritually. There is some area in their lives that torments them if they have not allowed the blood of Jesus to heal their broken heart.

The devastating thing about a child disconnected from the father is that you cannot predict what area of their lives will be affected or to what degree. But what I can predict is this: some area will be affected in a negative way. All through the Bible, both in the Old and New Testaments, fathers are given instructions concerning their children, far more instruction than is given to mothers. In Ephesians, the Holy Spirit speaking through the Apostle Paul commands,

> And you, fathers, do not provoke your children to wrath, but bring them up in the training and admonition of the Lord.
>
> Ephesians 6:4 NKJV

I find no Scripture that gives mothers this responsibility. This command coincides with the spiritual fact that the father is the nourisher of the children; he is commanded to bring them up and escort them to their destiny. A father can provoke his children to a negative state of mind. This negative life is triggered when men who are not mature enough to become escorts sow children into the earth, thus causing them to grow up bitter, angry, and discontent without their earthly father and no concept of a Heavenly Father. Disobedient fathers have disobedient children. Men who have no respect for women will pass this attitude on to their sons. Remember, men: everything reproduces after its own kind.

This reminds me of a relative of mine whom I knew was not escorted by his father. Yet, he acted just like his father; he had the character of his father without ever having extended contact with him. What was astonishing to me was how the sin nature of this father was manifested so much so that it appeared to be programmed into his child. The son got involved with the same type of crimes, had the same pattern of not raising his children, and was abusive towards women. A father without Christ will pass on his sin nature to his children.

Fathers must get born again in order to lead their children to God. When children grow up without God in their households, they are open to a lifestyle of sin. I do not mean a household where people just attend church; but where the Word of God is the standard for that household. Fathers, remember you are the first impression of God for your children. He made you in his image and his likeness. Children cannot afford to face life without you.,

Men, you can make an impact on the world if you first make an impact in your house. You may think your role in the earth realm is insignificant. What you produce into our communities makes up our communities; what you produce into society, makes up society; what you produce in our country, makes up our country.

Men, we have the power to affect our world one

child at a time. I trust you can see your role is critical to your child's wholeness and the world in which we all have to live. Fathers, you may think, "I don't agree with the premise you are basing your statements on. children will find their own way in life." Well, the Word of God is the principle I'm basing my facts on. In the book of Proverbs we read,

> "The righteous man walks in his integrity; his children are blessed after him."
>
> Proverbs 20:7, NKJV

This book is written to the believer. As a Christian, you are viewed as righteous by God, or as being in right standing with him.

As a result of my life being washed in the blood of Jesus, I am now capable of living a life of integrity. I find it quite interesting that God says a righteous man can now walk in integrity, and he then ties this to the man's children.

A father must have integrity. Father's need to be reliable, faithful, to have strength and courage, and to be honorable. Men, these traits are values your children need to draw from you in order to grow up whole. Children draw strength from their fathers when they know their father is faithful and reliable.

The prodigal son we looked at earlier in the chapter knew his father walked in integrity. Now notice in Proverbs 20:7 that the second half of that Scripture says the righteous man's children are blessed after him. Men, if you don't walk with God and in the blessing of God, your children cannot be blessed. Now, children may grow up, make a decision to receive Christ, and be blessed later in life. But there will be some drama and trauma while they make their own way to God.

Fathers, you can clear a path for your seed early on. We do not know how the challenges in life will affect each child. They may not get severely damaged by the experience of life without a father, or the experience may cause them a lifetime of discontentment, trying to find their roots.

God has a promise to godly fathers and their children, found in Psalms. Speaking through David, the Lord says,

> "I have been young, and now am old; yet have I not seen the righteous forsaken, nor his seed begging bread."
>
> Psalms 37:25, KJV

Fathers, as a result of your stand for God and your child, God says they will not live a life of begging. Now when you read this Scripture, you may immediately think of food, shelter, or clothing. It is true, children need those basic things to live. However, I believe the deeper revelation is they will not have to "beg" for a relationship with their Father. They will not have to beg for emotional support, attention, or love. Jesus said he is the bread of life. He was not referring to wheat, sourdough, or French bread. He was saying he is the main ingredient for spiritual life and everlasting life. Fathers, you are the main ingredient your children need to have a healthy, fulfilling life in the earth realm. Without a righteous man in a child's life, he will eventually find himself begging for relationship, begging for love, begging for strength, begging for nourishment—to live life whole and sound.

The word of God says,

> "All your children shall be taught by the Lord, and great shall be the peace of your children. In righteousness you shall be established; you shall be far from oppression, for you shall not fear; and from terror, for it shall not come near you."
>
> Isaiah 54:13–14 NKJV

Men, God has given you the assignment to teach your children about him. Notice that God says *great* shall be the peace of your children if you follow through on this. The righteous man, referring to the man in right standing with God, is mentioned again in verse fourteen. Fathers, if your seed has become disconnected from you, how will he find peace? You may say, "Pastor Stewart, how do you know God is talking to fathers in this Scripture and not mothers?" Well, we do know that Hebrew men were required to circumcise their sons, teach them a trade, and teach them about God. So we can, with certainty, say God is addressing the men in the context of this Scripture.

As a pastor, I have opportunity to look into the lives of the people of God. And, with the call on my life to the Christian family, I find myself time and time again ministering to the needs of children who themselves are living a life without the father.

There was this particular Christian teenage boy who was frequently being suspended from school, having contact with law enforcement, and, on one occasion, was up for expulsion as a result of physical violence against other students with gang affiliations.

Being a black man, I find myself in a similar situation as the Apostle Paul with his Hebrew brothers. Paul writes,

> "Brethren, my heart's desire and prayer to God for Israel is, that they may be saved. For I bear them witness that they have a zeal for God, but not according to knowledge."
>
> Romans 10:1, 2 NKJ

Too many black men have a zeal to make babies, but they are not armed with the knowledge that their seed needs them to grow and develop properly. A recent U.S. census statistical report stated seventy percent of black children in America are living in households without their fathers. It is no surprise that, in relationship to the number of African American men as a whole, the prison population in America is disproportionately housing over forty percent of African American men.

I have observed, firsthand, the mentalities and attitudes of many of these incarcerated men. Generally, these men had little or no contact with their fathers. They attribute their "wasted life" to a life without a father.

The Christian teenage boy referred to earlier is traveling the same path and is very likely to have the same result. I don't need a research study to prove this out; it is being lived out daily in our cities, communities, and all over the country.

I have made it my mission to try and steer him away from such a devastating life. In my heart, I know God can use me to influence him in a life of righteousness. But I know all too well, the principle of life without the father. As his pastor, I have shown him both love and concern. However, I know I'm not his father; there is no substitute for his father. This young boy is in emotional pain; he is a sheep without an escort. He is faced with the question, *Why did my father not want to escort me through life?* I see the question in his eyes every time I come in contact with him. Even though he has never asked the question verbally, I see the question in his eyes. Jesus said the eyes are the windows to the soul. This boy's soul is in despair; his soul is in disarray; his soul is disappointed that it cannot receive strength from the father. I would take this young boy shopping for clothing from time to time; his mother is a single parent with limited financial resources and couldn't always afford to supply the boy's clothing needs. On a particular occasion, I saw the boy and noticed his shoes were in really bad shape. I had my administrative assistant get in touch with his mom to get her permission to take the boy shopping. On our way to the mall, I inquired about his schoolwork, his behavior in school, and his walk with God. The young man was excited about his upcoming baseball playoff game. With optimism in his eyes, he asked, "Pastor, will you come to my game to see me play?" I went over my schedule and it was full; I had no time to attend a ball game. As a father, I attended my children's events. I can recall the confidence in their eyes when they would look in the stands and see their "strength giver," their "nourisher" there to support them. As a father, I made the commitment to my seed, "I can never leave you nor forsake you."

I would clear my schedule to make my children's events because I remembered how alone I felt when I would look into the crowd and not be able to find support. It was a constant reminder to me, "Clyde, you are living your life without the father."

I recall one high school track meet I asked my mother to attend. I knew she had to work to support six children, so normally I would not ask her to come to my events. She was off work this particular day and in a spur-of-the-moment manner, I asked, "Mom, could you come to my track meet today?"

I really didn't expect her to come, but to my surprise, she said, "Sure, I'll come."

I was so excited about the prospect of my mother showing up at my track meet that I could not fully concentrate on my event. I saw my mother sitting in her parked car—she did not come into the stands, but she watched me compete while looking through the chain link fence. I was a faster runner than my competition, but that day I did not care about winning. I ran my race, looking at my mother, and thinking, *Someone cared enough to come and see me.*

When this boy asked me to come to his game, the Holy Spirit brought that account to my remembrance and I told him, "Sure, I'll be there."

We went into the mall and he picked out a pair of shoes. The salesgirl asked him his shoe size. He replied, "A size eight, I think; the ones I have on are a size eight." I had the salesgirl measure his foot. His actual foot measurement was a size ten! This boy, disconnected from the father, was "squeezing" into a shoe that was two sizes too small and was willing to wear something that did not fit.

Children disconnected from the father will often "squeeze" into situations that don't fit a healthy lifestyle. They'll "squeeze" into teenage sex; they'll "squeeze" into drug or alcohol abuse; they'll "squeeze" into gangs or other criminal activity just to put something on.

Girls will often "squeeze" into unhealthy relationships with men in order to have a "father figure" in their lives. Although the figure does not fit, they'll "squeeze" into it nonetheless. In some cases, they think unhealthy attention is better than no attention at all.

I went to the young boy's game and when he entered the game, he looked into the stands and gave me a nod. I waved back and clapped my hands in approval of his turn at bat. He did not perform well that day. Later he said, "Wow, I had a bad game." I told him, "That's all right; you'll do better next time." I told him, "You looked a little too excited to compete, and you need to relax."

That's when the Holy Spirit reminded me of my track meet. The boy didn't really care about his performance; he was overwhelmed that someone cared enough to show up and watch him.

Fathers, if you have been remiss in your duties to show up, make a commitment before God to the seed you brought into the earth realm: I'll show up. You don't want your children "squeezing" into uncomfortable situations that can ruin their lives. Show up; your seed draws strength from its roots.

Since I'm on the subject of athletics, I find it most disheartening to hear testimony after testimony of struggling young men who had been brought up by loving, committed mothers. You observe these young men signing million-dollar contracts due to their superior athletic ability. When asked what the first thing they are going to purchase is, more often than not, when it is a black athlete, their response is, "I'm going to buy a house for my mother." She had such a hard time raising me and my brothers and sisters." These young men are instant millionaires on the outside, but they are often bankrupt on the inside.

We see millionaire athletes, rappers, actors, and actresses suffering through life, "squeezing" into bad situation after bad situation, often because of life without the father. I mentioned earlier how God brings real life research material across my path to authenticate my assertion.

A very famous multiple Grammy-award winner recently talked about his experiences of life without the father in an interview. The interviewer inquired about the performer's unusual name and asked how he came about it. The performer explained, "My father's mother died while giving birth to him, and I think that's who I was named after." The connection to the father had been broken at an early age, and the singer was not sure of his namesake. The singer also recalled when times were tough at home and life did not feel good, he would put on music. He'd said, "When my father left, he left a crate of records behind." This person's only connection to the father was music, and he held on to the one thing that nourished him and gave him strength: a crate of records touched by his father.

Although this person would be what society calls successful because of fame and fortune, he was not without his wilderness experience because of life without the father. The singer talked about his last CD, addressed his past drug and alcohol abuse, and the childhood abandonment by his father some thirty-six years ago. The man went through some pain and suffering that could have been avoided with a proper escort.

Praise God he found Jesus and states that he starts his day in prayer. I don't want to give the impression that an entire life will be wasted without the love of a father, but we can all agree some portions of life will be wasted without an escort. Simply put, there is no substitute for a father.

Jesus Had A Father

Now, we as believers and the world as a whole, know that Jesus was born to his virgin mother, Mary. Praise God for mothers and their obedience to God. God, being God, did not need or require a man to sow a natural seed in the womb of Mary to produce this child. If God had used a man to bring Jesus into the world, then Jesus himself would be in need of a Savior. Jesus would have inherited a sin nature, because that is the only nature natural man can give to their children.

So, God himself by his Spirit sowed an eternity-saving seed in the womb of Mary. The Bible records the birth of Jesus in Matthew 1:18, like this, "His mother Mary, was engaged to be married to Joseph. Before they came to the marriage bed, Joseph discovered she was pregnant. (It was by the Holy Spirit, but he didn't know that.) Matthew 1:18, note added.

Wow, what a shock! Joseph is thinking he is getting his promised virgin bride, and here she is pregnant. Joseph had to be following God's law of no unlawful sex before marriage, because the Bible says, "before they came to the marriage bed, he discovered she was pregnant."

Fathers, teach your children they are not to engage in sexual relations until they are married. Don't give in to the world's hypothesis that abstinence is not realistic. They are right, though; to a sinner, it is not realistic. But, to a believer, it is believable. I think if a father were to escort his seed through life that the child will obey the father's teaching and keep himself (or herself) from sexual sin. We know children will believe whatever a parent tells them and reinforces with strength to follow through. Children will believe in Santa Claus, the tooth fairy, Easter Bunny, etc. They grow up and find out these things are not true, because after they reach a certain age, it is no longer believable. If godly fathers will continue to live their lives for Christ, the children will grow up and discover that Jesus is real. *I see Jesus in my godly father. I can live this kind of life. It is not a fairy tale.* Men, if you will escort your children in holiness and righteousness, they won't depart from it when they grow old.

Florence and I did not smoke, drink, or use foul language toward one another, and our children grew up believing that this is normal Christian behavior. I recall a time when Charmaine was about six years old. We were at a restaurant; a couple seated at the table next to us were having alcoholic drinks with their dinner. I don't remember if they had a bottle on the table or not, but our daughter said, "Daddy, look! Those people are drinking!" She was so shocked and appalled at the sight, you would have thought the people were sticking needles in their veins. She had not seen mom or dad do this; she had heard mom and dad teach that this behavior is not godly. My two children are adults in their twenties and thirties now and do not consume alcohol or illegal drugs. They have shared with me the many opportunities and offers they have had to partake of such things, but life with a father taught them that this is not beneficial to your destiny.

You may think this to be simply brainwashing or extreme, but there is a history of alcoholism and substance abuse not only in my family, but also in my wife's family. We were not going to take a chance on this curse plaguing our children.

When Charmaine was in fourth grade, we lived in an "upper class" neighborhood; "good" homes, "good" community, "good" families … yeah, right. My daughter reported to me that two of her friends had stolen wine coolers from their parents' liquor cabinets and were passing the drinks around in the girls' bathroom at recess! Charmaine said she told the "peer pressure," "I will not take a drink of that; my father would get me if I do."

Well, I'm sure the other "grade" school girls had the same concerns; I'm sure their fathers would "get" them, too, if they knew they were consuming alcohol at school. But for some reason, for these girls it was not enough to deter the behavior. I contribute Charmaine's stand to having a godly escort that she knew was watching over her life.

When our seed know their father is God-like in their lives, they won't take the same risks as their friends. My daughter would walk home from school with her friends on a regular basis. I would, from time to time, pick her up and surprise her with a special date. We would go to the mall or just stop somewhere and eat. I was sowing precious time into her life. One day I had set aside time to surprise her by picking her up from school. On this particular day, school had already ended and the kids were already walking home. There was only one route Charmaine and her friends took to get to their homes. As I approached the street, I saw Charmaine and her friends walking down toward the gully. I blew my horn; Charmaine looked up and saw my car. She waved good-bye to her friends; she was being summoned by her escort. When she got in the car, I asked, "What were you girls doing down into the gully?"

She replied, "Oh, that's just a 'fun,' scary shortcut we take sometimes."

I told her, "Honey, daddy does not want you walking down there. It can be dangerous." Actually, the gully was a flood control ditch with some heavy brush and trees surrounding it.

I let her know, "There could be dangerous water down there, and there could be bad people there who will hurt little girls. Don't ever walk down there again." She promised me she would not walk in the gully ever again. I pretty much forgot about the incident until another time I went to pick her up and I saw her walking alone. I asked her, "Where are your other friends?"

She said, "They wanted to take the shortcut down in the gully, and I told them my father said it was not safe to walk down there." Now, Charmaine had no idea I would be picking her up on that day, as this was several weeks after she told me about the "shortcut."

Fathers, if you are an anointed escort for your seed, God will alert you of possible dangers to them. You, of course, must first have a relationship with God and be physically present in your child's life to receive this supernatural help.

Later we found out some girls had been injured in the gully. I was not glad to hear about this, but I praised God. Because of my stand, my child was saved from harm that could have impacted her throughout her adult life, causing her to have any number of other problems.

We first looked at Joseph, who discovered his fiancée-to-be was "with child" and it was not his. Joseph was not interested in becoming a "baby's daddy." He wanted to be a father. Joseph had thought about how he could cancel the relationship without making a public example of Mary. You might ask, "Well, they were not yet married; couldn't Joseph just walk away?"

In the Jewish culture, the marriage covenant was made about a year before the consummation of the marriage. It was during the one-year period of betrothal that Mary was found with child. Well, how did Joseph discover she was pregnant? If you search the Scripture, in Luke 1:36–56, Mary spent the first three months of her pregnancy with her cousin Elizabeth in Judea. When Mary returned to Nazareth, Joseph noticed, "Mary, you've put on a little weight since the last time I saw you."

Joseph wanted to divorce Mary on the grounds of infidelity. A divorce would be necessary because they had already made a marriage covenant, even though they had not yet known each other physically. Joseph could have made the divorce a public matter, or he could have gone through a private ceremony before two witnesses. Being a gracious and just man, Joseph decided to keep it private.

According to the Old Testament, if a man was taking a woman to be his wife as a virgin, and he found out that she was not a virgin, the husband would bring the woman to the door of her father's house, and the men of the city shall stone her to death with stones, because she had done a disgraceful thing in Israel—played the harlot in her father's house (Deuteronomy 22:21). I believe more fathers would endeavor to be escorts if the fate of their daughters having babies out of wedlock was stoning. Young teen girls having children without a husband is a type of death sentence to the child's full potential.

Now if you find yourself in this position or have daughters who have done this, I am not saying they will never reach their God-intended place. The forgiving blood of Jesus can restore all; however, an unplanned child with no husband or resources is a burden that will delay your destiny.

Joseph was not interested in hurting Mary, although I'm sure he was hurt that his wife had "stepped out" on him. I believe Joseph had an escort, a godly father who taught him about God. It would appear to me that Joseph was not plagued with emotional leaks. The average man might have wanted revenge; his ego would be hurt, and his very manhood challenged.

But Joseph was handpicked by God to fulfill his fatherhood role. What other kind of escort would God have picked out to guide Jesus through life? The Bible says Joseph was a righteous man, a man in right standing with God, a man whom God saw as a nourisher, protector, and strength giver to his son. God needed a man who would listen to him and not be intimidated or concerned about what other people thought. He would obey God in order to fulfill God's plan for his seed.

I'm sure, at the very least, family members were talking about how Joseph's wife, Mary, had returned from Judea pregnant. "I'll bet she was out running around, and Joseph is still going to marry her."

There are Scripture references where people called Jesus, "Mary's boy," insinuating we don't know who fathered Jesus. But God knew Joseph would fulfill his role as Jesus' escort. God didn't need Joseph to bring Jesus into the world, but God needed Joseph to escort Jesus through the world. If Jesus the Christ needed a father, don't you think your seed needs you?

Jesus was born to save mankind; his role was too vital to leave to a man who would not escort Jesus to his destiny.

Fathers, your seed has not been called to save mankind from sin, but your seed has a call to do something in the earth realm that only they can do. And you are the connection to their destiny, father. You ought to obey God.

The Bible reports Joseph's thoughts about how he could divorce Mary; instead, he got a divine message from God. Fathers, if you are willing to fulfill your duty as an escort, you will receive divine direction from God concerning your seed.

> An angel of the Lord appeared to him in a dream, saying, 'Joseph, son of David, do not be afraid to take to you, Mary your wife, for that which is conceived in her is of the Holy Spirit.'
>
> Matthew 1:20, NKJV

Remember, men: children are a gift from the Lord. You could say your child is of the Holy Spirit. Knowing this, how careful and watchful should you be with a gift from God? God had such confidence in this father to be, Joseph, that he told him what to name his son. Jesus means, "Yahweh is Savior." Hallelujah! We should be so thankful for Joseph's example of trusting God. The angel tells Joseph, "You shall call his name, 'Jesus.'" There is a bit of revelation to gain from this. Joseph was to name the child. If the father named the child, it meant he was claiming the baby as a member of his family. God had secured an escort for Jesus. Salvation was on its way; God using a man (Joseph) to help work out his plan of redemption. Praise God for Mary, but what about Joseph, the protector of God's seed?

Men, you are a vital part of God's plan for your children's safety and development. When King Herod got word the king of the Jews had been born, he set out to kill the destiny of Jesus. Herod is a type of Satan, trying to destroy children early on in life, so they will have a difficult time reaching the place God has for them. The Bible says the king gave a command to kill all boys ages two years old and under.

Fathers, if Satan can get a negative hold on our children early in their lives because you are not there, your seed will suffer through times of hurt and anger because they had no one to escort them to their place in God. Praise God that Joseph was there for Jesus, receiving divine direction.

> Angel of the Lord appeared to Joseph in a dream, saying, 'Arise, take the young child and his mother, flee to Egypt, and stay there until I bring

you word; for Herod will seek the young child to
destroy him.'

Matthew 2:13, NKJV

Now I'm sure this was hard on Joseph to just pick
up and leave his homeland in order to protect his
"son." Men, take note: Joseph did not hesitate to do
what was best for his "son." Joseph did not desert his
family because society was coming against him. Joseph
was a protector of his family, and he was there to stay.
Fathers, when you take a stand for your children, God
will take a stand for you. I submit to you that the gifts
the magi brought to Jesus were a divine deposit of
wealth to finance the trip to Egypt. The magi brought
gold; Joseph could not work his trade while he and the
family were on the move, so God rewarded him with
supernatural money to take care of his family. Jesus was
two years old; he didn't have any bills to pay. Joseph
was the head of the house, and God rewarded Joseph
for his obedience to care for his child. Joseph took the
young child and his mother by night and departed for
Egypt. There were no streetlights or police protection
for Joseph and his family; but God provided supernatural guidance for the journey.

Fathers, as you navigate the perils of life for your
family's journey; God will intervene on your behalf.
The Bible tells us when Herod was dead, an angel of
the Lord appeared in a dream to Joseph (not Mary)
saying, "Arise, take the young child and his mother,
and go to the land of Israel, for those who sought the
young child's life are dead" Matthew 2:20 (NKJV). Now
the path was clear for Jesus to fulfill his destiny, which
could not have come to pass without the earthly father,

Joseph. God is almighty; to be praised and glorified; he is the Alpha and the Omega. God worked his plan for Jesus with the assistance of Joseph.

Fathers, God's plan for your child will require your help and participation. Jesus' trade, as we all know, was that of a carpenter. Did Jesus learn this trade from God the Father? No. Jesus learned this trade from his earthly father, Joseph. Jesus is the Son of God—the only one ever begotten by God. But Jesus took on humanity to be our kinsman redeemer. He had to become like us in order to redeem us. Jesus had to sleep, eat, go to the bathroom, bathe, and grow up. Get rid of that religious Jesus and look at the real Jesus described in the Bible.

The Bible says in Luke 2:52 (NKJV), "Jesus increased in wisdom and stature, and in favor with God and men." Fathers, if you do not fulfill your role of an escort, you will damage the growth and development of your seed. I submit to you, if Joseph had not been a righteous man, Jesus could not have fulfilled his calling. And we have scriptural proof Joseph was escorting his responsibility, Jesus, through life.

The Bible tells us in Matthew 2:22 and 23, when Joseph received divine instruction to return to the land of Israel, he was afraid to go there because Archelaus was reigning over Judea instead of his father, Herod. Archelaus was a cruel, violent ruler; his behavior was so appalling the Roman government deposed him in AD 6 after a Jewish delegation took their protest to Rome. Joseph, being aware of Herod Archelaus' reputation, with guidance from God in a dream, turned north to Galilee. A father will inquire of God as to what is best for his child and believe me, God will provide divine direction.

Men, when you are missing from your child's life, they have no direction; their compass is missing, so they are vulnerable to the ills of sin and society. You are their savior from destruction; God will use you in a way that he cannot use their mother. I strongly believe Joseph's father, Jacob, was an escort who loved Joseph and trained him in the things of God. The seed of love and commitment sowed into Joseph's life by his father made an impact that benefited Jesus, the son of God.

The Scripture in Deuteronomy, that states a father's children's children will be blessed as the result of a father taking a stand for God, bears out truth. One's destiny is vital to one's fulfillment and success. If a father drops out of a child's life, that child's destiny is in jeopardy of being unfulfilled. I realize that God can restore and work out any challenge in our lives. But I also believe it is the will of God that our destiny not be delayed because an escort refused to lead his seed past the pitfalls of life.

The Bible prophesied Jesus' destiny was to come through the seed of David. Jesus could be physically of the line of David through Mary, but legally be the son of David through Joseph. If you study Scripture, you will find the genealogy brings Joseph to be a legal heir of David's throne. In the book of Matthew, however, he is careful not to identify Jesus as the physical son of Joseph. The Greek term translated "of whom" (Matthew 1:16) is a feminine singular pronoun that can only refer to Mary. But Joseph was handpicked by God to escort Jesus through his childhood. We can see that God was careful as to the type of man he allowed to be an influence on his son. Women must be careful when they marry a man to be their children's escort, because the man you choose can cause your children to win or lose in life.

Joseph, being obedient to God, settled in Nazareth. Nazareth was so obscure that it is never mentioned in the Old Testament. The village was considered an unlikely place for the Messiah to be raised. In the Gospel of John, Phillip invited Nathaniel to, "Come. We have found the Messiah." Nathaniel knew the Old Testament prophets had predicted that the Messiah would be born in Bethlehem. Nathaniel simply could not fathom that such a significant person as the Messiah could come from such an insignificant place as Nazareth. Nathaniel's reply to Phillip was, "Can anything good come out of Nazareth?" Yes, if they have the proper escort!

Fathers, it does not matter the color of your skin, or the city or country you live in. If, from the ghetto to the suburbs, you decide to guide your seed through the maze of sin and confusion in our society today, people will stand and take notice: "Look at the superb product that was produced from that place!" I hope you can see the importance of fathers. Jesus the Christ had an earthly father to learn from. Jesus learned from *his* earthly father. I mentioned earlier about Joseph's commitment to guiding his family to God; God did not just pick any Tom, Dick, or "Joseph" to raise his son. He handpicked Joseph to bring up his son in a lifestyle of godliness.

Herod massacred innocent children, trying to stop God's plan. Herod is a "type" of Satan. There are "Herods" in society today that have been massacring our children: liberalism, teenage pregnancies, abortions, substance abuse, gang violence, child pornography, molestations, and rapes perpetrated by sin-sick adults. If Satan can cause some emotional trauma early on in our children's lives, he will delay or destroy their destiny.

Joseph took his role seriously; he had Jesus circumcised on the eighth day as the law required (Luke 2:21). According to the law of Moses, after the days of Mary's purification, Joseph took Jesus to Jerusalem and presented him to the Lord.

Notice this; here is Jesus the Son of God being presented to the Lord! The Lord of lords being presented to the Lord! It wouldn't make any sense to do this, except to show us it takes a father to lead his child to God. God was using Joseph to show us, "If my son's development was dependent upon an earthly father, your sons' and daughters' development is dependent upon an earthly father."

I realize Joseph was following the Lord, but a deeper spiritual truth was also in play: a natural man, Joseph, fulfilling the plan of a supernatural God. It takes the natural, in subjection to the supernatural, to get what God has predestined to come to pass.

God has predestined children to have an escort in their lives. Joseph was escorted correctly; he had been taught, "Every male who opens the womb shall be called holy to the Lord," because that male child will one day grow up and become an escort himself. The Bible tells us Joseph waited the forty-day purification period after the mother's flow of blood before he came and made a sacrificial offering of two pigeons to God.

Now when Joseph and Mary were at the temple they received a word concerning the destiny of Jesus (Luke 2:33–34). Women, be careful of the man you choose to escort your children. If he doesn't want to go to church to praise God and be taught the Word, that man is not for you. If he doesn't think it is vital to belong to a spirit-filled, Word-teaching church, your children will miss out on divine direction from God. Don't measure a man by the color of his skin, his educational background, his stock portfolio, or his good looks—none of these will give you a glimpse into his character. Your barometer should be, "is he following God in his own personal life so that I can submit myself and my future children to him?"

Joseph took his family to Jerusalem for the feast of the Passover; Jesus was then twelve years old, and a godly lifestyle had been stamped in his natural mind to go along with his divine nature. Jesus' spirit was housed in a flesh and blood body like yours and mine. If Jesus didn't have a natural body, he could not have died for our sins. So, because Jesus had a natural body, he could have yielded to sin and disqualified himself as the Messiah. Part of God's plan was to have a man, Joseph, watch over his son. Generally, whole extended families would travel together to the feast. Because of the large crowd of people, Mary and Joseph did not notice Jesus had stayed behind in Jerusalem. It took them three days to find him, and I'm sure Joseph must have felt terrible that his "son" had been left behind.

Fathers, if your heart is right toward God, he will cover your mistakes with the very blood of this Jesus, whom his earthly father Joseph was going to locate. The Bible says they found him in the temple, in church! What an awesome job Joseph had done escorting Jesus. Jesus was not hanging out on the corner; he was not in juvenile hall; he had not done a drive-by shooting;

he was not at his girlfriend's house—he was in church. Praise God!

Now you may say, "Well, that was Jesus. What would you expect?" The Bible tells us he was tried, tempted, and tested like we are; so Jesus could have been "hanging out," getting into trouble. But no, his father had brought him up right. Jesus was in church.

How did they know to look in the temple? Jesus was now twelve years old; he must have displayed a strong interest in the things of God for Mary and Joseph to look for him there. So, Mary asked the question,

> Son, why have you done this to us? Look, your father and I have sought you anxiously.
>
> Luke 2:48, NKJV

It takes a man and a woman to meet the standards of God when it comes to children. If you are a single parent, God's grace will help you. If you don't have any children, make a decision: I will raise my children based on God's highest standard. Please don't get the impression I am booting mothers out of the process; I'm merely magnifying God's order.

Fathers are the roots to a child's success in life. Joseph was just as anxious about Jesus' well-being as was Mary. Jesus was now at the age when intensive instruction for him begins in preparation for the age of responsibility. At age thirteen, when a boy was accepted into the religious community as a man, he was responsible to keep the law.

The answer Jesus gave to his mother and father in reply to Mary's question to him was a most unusual response,

Why did you seek me? Did you not know that I must be about my Father's business?

Luke 2:49, NKJV

The Greek text is elliptical here and reads, "I must be in the ... of my Father," without specifying a place or activity. Either Jesus must be about the Word of God, as the translation suggests, or he must be in the house of God, discussing God's truth. I like the latter translation because Scripture says,

> "They found him in the temple, sitting in the midst of the teachers, both listening to them and asking questions. And all who heard him were astonished at His understanding and answers."

Luke 2:46–47, NKJV

So, unlike traditional teaching, Jesus was not lecturing or arguing with the rabbis, but rather engaging the rabbis in theological discussions. I'm sure Mary and Joseph probably caught some of Jesus' questions and answers; however, they were not impressed. They were typical of moms and dads, concerned about the safety of their child. Fathers, when you take your rightful place as the head of your family, you will find your seed interested in the things of God and being consumed with their father's business, godliness, holiness, and righteousness.

Children being raised in this type of climate will not fall prey to the so-called MTV or Generation X syndromes. There was no way Almighty God was going to risk his plan of redemption on an irresponsible, non-God-fearing man. He could not afford to have the Savior of the world grow up with emotional leaks or some psychological dysfunction or behavior. God's plan was so specific that the prophet spoke in Judges 13:5, "He *(referring to the Messiah)* shall be called a Nazarite." God needed Joseph to obey him and trust him that he was bigger than King Archelaus, return his son to the region of Galilee, and eventually dwell in a city called Nazareth. God's plan for your seed is so specific that God needs fathers to obey him so he can work out his plan for your child's development and destiny. It is easier for God to work with your child when he or she has grown in an environment where Jesus is Lord.

In Matthew chapter three, we find Jesus stepping into his destiny. The Word tells us that Jesus came from Galilee to the Jordan River to be baptized by John. Jesus could have had some emotional hang-ups or low self-esteem and told John, "I am the Messiah. I don't need to be baptized."

Jesus was not afraid to humble himself just because he was Messiah. Jesus was in submission to the Father and told John, "It is fitting for us to fulfill all righteousness." Jesus was so stable and functional; he had no problem pleasing God. It was more important to him to fulfill his destiny than yield to some fleshly whim.

When God saw his son's stability and obedience, the Bible says a voice from heaven said, "This is my beloved Son, in whom I am well pleased" (Matthew 17:5, NKJV). I submit to you that if Joseph had not fulfilled his role as a strength giver to Jesus, God's plan for redemption would have been in "jeopardy." You may say, "Pastor Stewart, God had everything under control." Yes, I agree God has everything in his power under control. However, when God is working through human agents, man's will is involved, and God does not violate our wills to "make" us obey him.

Let's look at the Bible's account where Satan took Jesus up on an exceedingly high mountain and showed him all the kingdoms of the world and their glory. Satan said to Jesus,

> All these things I will give you if you will fall down and worship me.
>
> Matthew 4:9, NKJV

Well, Jesus could have yielded to the temptation, or it would have been no temptation to him. Jesus' will was involved. Joseph's and Mary's wills were involved in their obedience to God. So, don't get super-spiritual or off-base that God's plan is automatic. God works through people and he needs their participation. Without Joseph's participation in raising Jesus, our Lord and Savior would have had some human issues to deal with, just like any other boy or girl who experienced life without the father. Because of Joseph escorting his children, they were a close-knit, functioning family. In Scripture, we have an account of Jesus' brothers and Mary seeking to talk to him; they wanted to tell him to stop all this preaching and teaching about being the Son of God because even his own brothers, the Bible says, did not believe in him. Notice who was absent from this assault: Joseph, his father and nourisher. He remembered how God had directed him and Mary. Joseph remembered the divine intervention. He knew the diligent effort he had deposited in Jesus' life as a child. Now that Jesus was a grown man who had been escorted by the father, Joseph had every confidence that his son was following God's plan for his life.

Fathers, when you properly escort your child, as they grow older, they won't be perfect. But I can assure you that they won't fall into an emotional ditch, which could take years before they emerge; neither will they be dysfunctional or a danger to society. They will know, "I had a father who loved me and developed me so that I would not have to face life alone or search for the answer to a lifelong question, 'Why wasn't I valuable to my father?'" God knew the enormity of this connection, which is why Jesus had a father.

There Is No Substitute for a Father

Behold, children are a heritage from the Lord.

Psalms 127:3 NKJ

Children are a gift from God. God has placed your children in your life so that you can train them in righteousness and direct them to God. When children misbehave, it may seem like they are from Satan. But the Bible says they are from God.

Now, since the word of God is true, I must accept that my child is from God; so what effort am I to put into a "gift" from God?

The responsibility of a Jewish father was to see that his son was circumcised; had the sign of covenant; learned a trade so that he could provide for himself and his future family. The father was to teach his children about God, to recite to his children God's faithfulness and goodness.

Now, men, listen. The choices you make concerning a life with or without God are not only going to affect your children, but your children's children. Children are designed to respond to a father in a way of reverence. That's different than how they respond to mother. I mentioned before about my career in corrections. In counseling, inmates and others (who were not incarcerated) would tell me growing up without a father and being disciplined by a mother only. They had little or no fear (reverence) of their mother's ability to hand out punishment or to enforce it. They loved their mothers, but they knew she could only discipline them up to a certain age.

A youth is not likely to challenge a man's authority as he would a woman's. Children and adults just view men in a different light. When children deal with dad, their tone generally takes on a different tenor. Your grandchildren are more likely to be healthier emotionally if your children are emotionally healthy. You are raising a person who will someday become a husband or wife. How will their spouse enjoy or disdain the mate you raised for them? Future marital bliss or turmoil will arise as a result of the stability you have developed in the seed that is currently in your household—under your authority. Your children's ability to love their spouses results from the love you cultivated in them. Because you first loved them, your children's capacity to love themselves (and others) will be apparent. Remember, father, in a child's eyes, you are God.

A child cannot grow up to be an affectionate, loving husband or wife if they are not satisfied with their personal self-worth, which can be damaged by life without a father. When a female child has grown up with a loving, godly father, she will know what kind of man to accept into her life. A boy will know how to be a man because he lived with one; not just every other weekend, during the summer, and on holidays, but because he lived with a father and learned by example how to be a father.

On Father's Day in 2000, my son called me and said, "Happy Father's Day. Thank you for teaching me to become a man. Thank you for showing me what it is to be a man. Thank you for spanking me. Thank you for fussing at me. Thank you for not letting me have my own way. Thank you for not letting me go to all the places I wanted to go. Thank you, thank you for staying with my mother." He went on to say, "You made me what I am today. I am so glad I don't have any children out of wedlock; I've never been arrested; I've not used drugs or alcohol. Thank you for teaching me about God. I have a good start on life because of you, because of the decision you made to serve God. Dad, my sister and I missed a lot of huge setbacks because of your stand with God. Charmaine and I have self-confidence because of the love you deposited in us. We didn't give in to peer pressure and go along with the crowd, because you escorted us through life." Those words, coming from my adult son, brought life to the Scripture found in Proverbs,

> Train up a child I the way he should go; and when is old he will not depart from it.
>
> Proverbs 22:6, NKJV

Many times in black communities you will find substance abuse, gang violence, school dropouts, and teenage pregnancy; we have a tendency to blame these ills on society. I take a different view of the problem. It is not society's fault for what we develop (or don't develop) in our children. It is the lack of a father in a household that causes all the failures we see in our cities (inner city or suburbs). If a father is not escorting his child, that child is destined for failure. Income status will not matter; it's just that low-income people's social failures seem to surface earlier in life, and are magnified by society. When you put forth your best godly effort into your child, they will miss the ills of society that plague others who have not had a life escort.

Fathers, when you escort your children, you are placing what I call "preventive guards" in their lives. The medical profession is now very proactive in endorsing preventive measures for us to take that will prevent disease from attacking our bodies. Fathers, if you will escort your children through life, you will prevent them from making major mistakes that can cause them years of pain and trauma. It is better to learn beforehand what causes failure than to make a poor decision and have to try and recoup lost years of destruction that could have been years of productivity. Experience is not the best teacher.

I got my wife pregnant when she was sixteen. Experience taught us that that was not the best way to start off our lives. I taught my children the principle that "experience is not the best teacher" so that they would not have to learn from a life-altering experience. Experience will teach you something; but it's far better to have a life escort instruct you than to experience years of regret.

You may hold the opinion, "Well, kids need to experience and learn for themselves." Not so. My daughter did not need the experience of being a mother at age sixteen; it is too difficult being a teenage mom. My son did not have to experience being a seventeen-year-old dad. Instead, they learned being a teenager is a time to grow and enjoy life as a child, not to try and raise a child. The curse of teenage pregnancy had been in my family line for generations. I broke the cycle of teen pregnancy in my own family by escorting my children through their teen years. As a result of taking a godly stand in my children's lives, through God I became capable of escorting them around the pitfalls that still plague so many families today.

You do not know what a particular individual's outcome will be because of their experiences. Some abuse drugs and alcohol and never recover; some have children out of wedlock and never get an opportunity to escort their own children. Place preventive guards in the life of the seed you are responsible for. There are some things that children can learn on their own and grow from. However, there are life-altering issues that your seed needs guarding against. Father, you are the lifeguard. Life is going to demand that you be either an escort or observer. You must answer the demands that life will try and put on your seed. I like the Greek definition of a father. It's the word, pater. Pater means to provide your children with things that are necessary to life, healthy growth, and development. It also means to promote one's children. Father, your seed will not be able to make it to the next grade in life if you do not provide the things they need that cause them to grow and develop into emotionally stable persons. Traditionally, most men have primarily been the breadwinners of the house. However, most men have not taken on the demand of the nourisher of their seed; i.e., the primary one who helps promote them throughout life. Too often promoting children has been left to mothers. It takes a father's guidance first—with the help of the child's mother. Women, don't take this as a putdown; this is God's order. Men are to be the head of the house. God gave woman to man to *help* him. And ladies, we do need your help. We cannot do it alone. However, we are designed to take the lead.

Mothers are invaluable. They have the ability to access both sides of their brains. Men, on the other hand, spend the majority of their lives on the logical side of their brains. Women, you help to keep us balanced.

Fathers, I mentioned in an earlier chapter that you are the *nourisher* of the children. The word 'nourisher' is a part of the definition linked to the word vitamin. Americans are big on vitamins; we take vitamins because we believe they will give us nourishment that will help our bodies stay healthy and strong. Well, fathers, you are the emotional nourishment (vitamin) your seed needs if it is gong to be healthy and reach its full potential. We take vitamins because they cause our bodies to function and operate at its optimal level. Well, fathers, without you, your child will not be capable of operating at his optimal level. Vitamins give us confidence that we are promoting a healthy body. Father, when you are involved in your child's life, it builds their confidence. It causes them to draw strength from your commitment to them. Your seed may not be the smartest child or the most talented child; but if your child has been nourished correctly, they will succeed where the brightest, most talented child failed, because they did not have an escort to nourish their life.

Fathers, to make this kind of impact on your child will cost you a price. It's going to cost you time, energy, and a change in your priorities. Men, your family is going to have to be your primary concern. Not your career; not your golf game; not your lawn—but the seed you sowed in the earth realm. Father, what value is your six-figure income when the relationship with your child does not add up? What is the value in having the best-looking lawn in the neighborhood and losing your family? We had a neighbor once who spent countless hours working on his lawn, day in and day out. He had a wife and two beautiful little girls. One day, I noticed his house was up for sale. When I inquired about their move, to my dismay, I was told they were divorcing. I thought to myself, *How tragic. I wonder if he had put the same put effort into cultivating his family that he put into cultivating his beautiful and immaculate yard, what his family's future would be.* And the beautiful yard he spent so much time tending? Sadly, someone else would now reap the benefit and enjoyment of all his hard work and effort.

How can you brag about your devotion to your golf game or your last spectacular fishing trip while your seed is being caught up in the ills of sin? Men, take a sober look at your own situation and the longing you had for your father's attention, time, and approval. Your seed needs you.

Now, men, there is nothing wrong with being successful in the business world, but not at the expense of the wholeness of your child. If you are reading this book and you and your wife are thinking about having children, ask yourself, "Am I ready to change the priorities in my life?" If not, you are not yet ready to become an escort. If you are able to provide for your children the extras in life, but it costs you not having quality time for your child, your seed is going to suffer.

In the late eighties, the first pair of Air Jordan athletic shoes was introduced in the sports world. I recall my son wanting a pair; the price tag was a whopping $89.00! Well, I was financially able to provide them for my son, and he still remembers being the first one on the block with the coveted Air Jordans.

Yet my son tells me one of his fondest memories was of us as a family going on an overnight camping trip; his fishing line got caught on a tree and the two of us reached and tugged on the line. Finally, he tripped and fell into the lake, fully clothed! What a laugh we had! In other words, that camping trip that I took the time to take him on was more valuable to him than my providing him with the prestige of being the first kid on the block with Air Jordans.

Father, you should be your child's hero, not some stranger on TV or in the entertainment field. Owning video games, iPods, the latest clothes, bikes, or tennis shoes do not translate love to a child. A hug; a kind word; a bedtime story; accompanying your child's class on a field trip; your connection tells your seed, "I love you. You are worth my time."

The welfare system cannot raise healthy children. The government may send your child a check, food stamps, and a medical sticker, but they cannot tell your child, "You are priceless; you are important." The government can't tell your children about Jesus; as a matter of fact, the government and schools are likely to be opposed to Jesus. But father, you are supposed to escort them to Christ. Remember men you are a pater; the one who provides for your seed the things that are necessary to life spiritually, emotionally, and physically.

Fathers, it is impossible to provide emotional stability for your child if you are not physically present. You may send child support payments, but if you do not have continual physical involvement in the lives of your children, you are not supplying all their needs. Your children may have a roof over their heads, but without you in their lives, they will have a hole in their hearts.

When people grow up without their escorts, they develop a void in their hearts. They go their whole lives searching for anything to fill that void. It's like sinners without Christ in their lives; they try and find substitutes for God. And we who are saved know there is no substitute for God. There is no substitute for you either; you are your child's connection to this life. If you become disconnected, your seed cannot grow into what it would have been if it had stayed connected to its roots.

Father, there is no substitute for you; you are designed by God to protect your children. Another part of the definition of a pater is a *defender*. Fathers, you are designed by God to shield your seed from harm. Harmful habits, harmful people, and harmful emotional distress can cause them to grow up with *leaks* in their souls. Fathers, you cannot defend what you have separated from; it is imperative that you stay connected to the seed you sowed into this life. When my seed, Anthony, was about five years old, there was a bully at the apartment complex where we lived. He was two years older than the other boys. He would take their toys and take cuts on the swings and other rides in the play area. Anthony would come to me crying, complaining about the playground bully. As his protector, I had to teach him that he had to stand up for himself. In life, there will be people who will misuse you, if you allow it. Now, I grew up "in the hood." At the time I was a young father, and I was not born again, but I was a protector of my seed. I took my seed aside and told him to ball up his fists and punch my hand. I put his little arms in a fighting stance and showed him how to put up his dukes, as we called it in my day. I told my son, "The next time the bully tries to hurt you, let him know that you will protect yourself." I gave him confidence that with pater on your side, you can face any fight in life. Well, Anthony went back to the playground and put the plan into action. The bully left him alone. Just to show you the impact that we have on our seed, to this day at age thirty-six, my son will not back down from a fight. I'm not proud that he will not back down from a fight, but I am proud I was instrumental in giving him the confidence to stand up for himself.

You must understand at the time that was the best plan I could devise to protect my seed. If I had been absent, I believe he would be at a disadvantage today when it comes to a foundation belief that, "I am valuable to my father; he took the effort to show me how to protect myself."

In chapter one, I mentioned my own personal disconnection from my father. He left our family when I was eight years old. I remember myself in a similar situation with a bully. I had no one to turn to for help or advice. So I hid and took the long way home so as not to encounter the neighborhood bully. One Saturday I was sitting on my porch, afraid to go down the street to play with the other kids. There was this teenage big brother figure that lived across the street from us. We called him Sonny Boy. He stopped by and asked, "Clyde, why aren't you out playing ball with the other kids?" I reluctantly told him about the boy who was picking on me. Sonny Boy asked me, "Don't you know how to fight?" I told him I didn't have anyone to teach me. Like a trained fighter preparing an amateur for battle, Sonny Boy looked me in the eye and said, "Clyde, ball up your fists, put your arms up like this, and punch my hands." I began to feel a slight sense of confidence come over me; enough to stand up to the bully, but not enough to face him. Sonny Boy had done an admirable job of helping me face my fear, but Sonny Boy was not my pater. I went back into the house to stay out of the path of the bully. I was disconnected from the father and could not find the strength to face my fear. From that point on, I found myself being a loner; introverted and sharing my feelings and concerns with myself, the only person I thought I could count on. It took me decades to learn to believe in myself. God had placed some awesome gifts and talents in my life that were delayed as a result of life without the father. Each child is affected differently from this traumatic experience.

Take my older brother for example; he was outgoing, popular, and an extrovert. He later grew up to have numerous contacts with law enforcement. He too was disconnected from the father.

Father, a function of your root system to your seed is to provide strength for someone who is weaker than you. As a father, you are designed to uphold them, carry them, and give them support. Your children are weaker than you and cannot protect or support themselves. Now, it is obvious they cannot support themselves financially, but it is just as important to note that they cannot support themselves emotionally. As a child, I was an emotional wreck. I needed some emotional support because I had been disconnected from my father's "root system"! Fathers, don't leave your seed unprotected.

If you are reading this book and find yourself wondering about your emotional ability to love yourself and others, go back to your root system to discover if this was the start of the emotional leak in your life. Allow God to put your soul in order and move on to what God had planned for your life all along.

If you are a father who is thinking about leaving, disconnecting from your seed; stop and think, "I'm responsible for the development of my seed." Your children will pay a high price for your selfishness if you run out on them just because things are bad between you and their mother. Emotionally, they can't afford it. With God's intervention you can save your seed years of internal searching and wondering, "What is missing in my life?" Fathers, you must do everything in your power to make a commitment to your child.

Father, if you use the strength that God placed in you to be a pater, your seed can draw strength from you to overcome life's obstacles. I like using real life situations to prove out the Word of God. Again, I will use my seed as an object lesson.

To further his pursuit in his career of choice, Anthony had to go through a lengthy stay at an academy that included a grueling training course. He told me how difficult the long days were; the classroom work; the physical demands of the training. He told me about the strict rules of the training and how the company did all it could to weed out weak people: people who were physically weak, emotionally weak, or weakened by character flaws. He then told me about candidates who had been dismissed for behavioral reasons, for violating the code of conduct, and for failing the classroom and physical requirements of the academy. He said there were several times he wanted to quit; he wanted to give up. There was one particular time when a superior really got in his face and tried to get him to crack.

My seed said he thought about me and how he felt I would have handled this intense pressure. He said he drew strength from my example of sticking out tough situations.

Father, if your seed did not have a physical and emotional connection to you, they will find themselves reaching for help, only to realize they have nothing to hold on to. Their likelihood of being productive will be diminished as a result of life without the father.

Father, you may look at your little ones and not realize you are producing a product. Your seed will grow and become a commodity in society. Will you put a product into society that will help our world become a better place to live in? Or, because your seed was disconnected from you, society has to live with the nightmare of your failure as a pater.

When I read the newspaper or talk to others about the ills of America and see the reckless and irresponsible actions of people, I cannot help but think, *What kind of escort did this person have or not have, in life?* Because of my assignment, God is constantly placing things across my path to confirm the revelation that *fathers are life escorts.*

There was an article in the newspaper about a six-teen-year-old boy who had shot and stabbed his victim. Now, you would think shooting *or* stabbing a person would have been devastating enough; but why do both? The boy was up for sentencing when his father, in another city, read the article about the crime. The father said he almost fell out of his seat when he read the perpetrator's name. It was his son, whom he had abandoned years ago. That's not all. The father, himself, when he was sixteen had committed the same type of crime and was incarcerated for it. The father was riddled with guilt and lamented that he felt badly for not raising his son and teaching him to become a more productive person.

> Behold, children are a heritage from the Lord.
> The fruit of the womb is a reward. Like arrows in
> the hand of a warrior, so are the children of one's
> youth.
>
> Psalms 127:3–4 NKJV

This boy was caught in the heritage of the curse, with no God in his life and no father to guide him. The Bible tells us every seed reproduces after its own kind. Personally, I grew up with a friend who was involved with shooting a person; later his son (whom he did not escort) grew up and went to prison for shooting someone.

Hear my children the instructions of a father, and give attention to know understanding.

Proverbs 4:1, NKJV

Men, if you are not there to give your seed instructions, they will get wrong information from other sources. And you are the one with their instructions; not society; not a stepfather; not the government; not the school system; but their father.

Looking back, Psalms 127:4 likens children to arrows in the hand of a warrior. A good warrior knows the importance of a functional arrow. If the arrow is slightly bent, it will not fly accurately or hit its target. Or, if the arrow does not have a sharp point, it cannot penetrate its target. Fathers, you are the marksman for your children's future. There are three parts to an arrow: the shaft, the tip, and the feather on the tail to guide it. Like the arrow, there are three parts to our nature; spirit (tip), soul (feathers), and body (shaft). Your children will be ineffective in some area of their lives because they did not have a "marksman" to maintain their flight pattern into society. Notice the Bible calls the father a "warrior." As I mentioned earlier, men, you are going to have to battle for your seed's success in the earth realm. You are going to have to protect them in the earth realm. There are so many negative influences pulling on our children today. Teachers are becoming involved in sexual relationships with students at an alarming rate; drugs and alcohol are epidemic; and among young people, AIDS is on the rise in teenagers.

Father, you must stand up and fight for your seed's survival in a perverse world. When children are dealing with peers and society, they are immature, insecure, and unstable. This is the natural process of maturation. Every person goes through his or her growth stages. Therefore, every person needs an escort if they are to exit these stages as a whole and stable person.

Children will have temptations and choices to make in life. I am not suggesting that you can shield every temptation your child will have to face. But you can be the strength and information system they use to make their choices.

I do not believe that our schools or government should teach our children about sex education other than giving them biological facts. Fathers should teach their children about keeping themselves from sexual activity. It is not the school's place to teach our children about condom use, abortions, or sexual orientation. The father living in the home with a mother can give a child both perspectives about sex. Today's society is bombarded with sex. It will take the strength of a father to keep his seed safe from liberal perspectives about sexual activity. Father, if you don't teach your seed about sex, the Internet or some other ungodly source will. Remember, you are to give your children instructions. Godly fathers teach their children "safe sex" is only between married people; putting a condom on does not make sex safe.

Fathers, part of my definition of a father means to camouflage their seed, much as an animal would protect its young in the wilds of the jungle. Fathers are so close to the needs of their seed that if danger shows up, it will have to cross the path of the father. Danger will not see an unprotected child that can be exploited by sin.

We had a dating rule in place for our children; they

could not date while they were in high school. They were allowed to go to school functions, friends' parties, movies, etc., but as far as having an exclusive relationship with another teen, as in "girlfriend" or "boyfriend," it was not allowed. It was my responsibility to watch over my seed.

One situation comes to mind that again involves my son when he was, I'd say, a freshman in high school. One Saturday afternoon, our doorbell rang. I answered the door to see approximately six young girls standing on our porch. I greeted them and asked, "May I help you?" The girl leading the group asked if Anthony was home—girls travel in protective packs at this age. I called Anthony to the door and said, "Some girls are here to see you." I did not give him the "wink, wink—way to go, son" glance of approval, nor did I feel proud that my son "had it going on with the ladies, a chip off the old block." No, I asked him who the girls were and to introduce me to them. As the girls began to give their names, there was this one girl kind of hiding in the back. And all the girls said, "This is 'so and so,' Anthony's girlfriend." I calmly replied, "Oh no. She can't be Anthony's girlfriend; he is not allowed to have girlfriends."

I did not want to give my son the impression he was making me proud by having girls come over to our house. Now, I realize it is natural for boys and girls to be attracted to each other. However, I felt it was vital to his protection that I reiterate one-on-one, girlfriend and boyfriend dating relationships are not safe for teens. Fathers, there are adults who cannot successfully "date" without compromising their Christian values. Can we honestly expect teens to be involved in relationships and not get into trouble? I was not trying to be rude or insensitive to the young girl's feelings, but my job as an escort is to support and promote what is best for my seed. I gave my son the reassurance, "I know what is best for you. I possess wisdom concerning your life." To be an effective escort, one must be sensitive and sympathetic to the vulnerability of children. Children are fragile and vulnerable, so, fathers, you must be their man of steel. Fathers, you are your children's superhero, their support system in the earth realm. Previously I likened children to a product that will be placed on the shelves of society. In business, products are promoted as having certain qualities that will make your life better. If we as fathers were to promote our children as valuable commodities that will one day make life better for others, we will see fewer and fewer adults with emotional leaks that are being passed on from generation to generation. When boys would stop by our house and ask for Charmaine, I would give them a firm handshake, thus letting them know she has a hands-on father. I'm here to escort my daughter through her teen years. I mentioned earlier teens don't possess the maturity to date. Most teens date due to peer pressure or a life without the father. I recall a time when my daughter was distressed after one of her friends had been assaulted by her boyfriend. The girl did not want to do a particular thing the boyfriend wanted her to do, so he physically assaulted her, stating, "You are my girlfriend, and you will do what I want." This poor girl, I would imagine, did not have an escort, or she would not have been so emotionally attracted to this boy.

I would take my son and his friends to L.A. Rams football games and other events; he had a set group of friends who were into sports. On one such trip, I noticed one of the boys was no longer going with us; mind you, these boys are in tenth and eleventh grades. I asked, "Where is 'so and so'?" The boys told me, "Oh, he can't go. His girlfriend told him that she would be mad at him if he went." Now, I knew the boy and his family, and I can tell you he had lived his entire life without an escort. He had many girlfriends, two children out of wedlock, caused a person's death while driving drunk, and eventually wound up in prison for manslaughter. As a result of being disconnected from the father, his destiny, gifts, and talents would not be realized while he was sitting in a jail cell.

Men, your children need to learn values and morals from a godly father. Athletes, entertainers, and even politicians should not be role models for your seed. You don't want to encourage your seed to be like this "star" or that "athlete" if you do not know their moral standards. And really, how can we know what a person stands for or what they believe in simply because they can hit a home run, slam dunk a basketball, or bring you to tears singing a song? You should endeavor to be the model of a man who shows his male seed how a godly man lives and to model for his female seed what to look for in a husband. This is the character you want in the man who will escort your children through life. I know some may read this and think, "Does this man realize we are now in the twenty-first century?" Yes, I realize the times we are living in; that's why I'm so passionate about fathers (men), taking a stand for righteousness concerning their seed. We have to deal with and face so many burdens in our society because of the type of products coming out of homes in America. The boys, who bring guns to school and terrorize communities, came out of a man; they came from a household. They did not come from Mars or Jupiter, but from a household; and more often than not, without an escort.

We in society have to pay for it with our dollars to lock them up, raise them in juvenile facilities, or even with the very lives of our loved ones.

My ministry is in San Bernardino County. This county leads the state of California in sending people to prison. Despite these sobering statistics, murders, drug addiction, and teenage pregnancy remain a serious problem in this county.

A father who is present in a family has the opportunity to protect and develop his seed. He is the warrior, with his children in his hands as arrows, giving them support for a life that will hit the targets of success, thus making our cities and nation safe and godly.

Men, those children in your house are growing and being influenced daily. You don't have a moment to lose. If you have not taken your responsibility seriously, start now. Don't put it off another day. While you are pondering, "Should I be more aggressive in my child's development?," the Internet or some drugged-out singer or movie star is having an influence on your seed. The entertainment industry is only concerned about dollars and cents. They have little or no concern about the type of negative impact they are having on our society.

A few years ago, cigarette advertisers had to be told, "Stop making ads that are enticing to children." You would think rational businessmen would be concerned about how their adult product might be enticing to youth. We live in a capitalistic country where the bottom line is profit. I love our country; I would not want to live anywhere else. Capitalism gives every person a shot at making a profit. With this in mind, fathers, endeavor to be the protector of your seed. It is not the duty or concern of big businesses to protect your children. Companies are in business to make money. If their businesses destroy lives, so be it, as long as they make a profit for their shareholders.

Drinking among teenagers, as well as young adults in colleges, is at an all-time high. Recent reports have been published pointing out how colleges ought to take a more proactive role on their campuses concerning the problem of student drinking. One reporter even implied school presidents were looking the other way and not facing the challenge of on-campus drinking. He went on to say all the school cared about was academic and financial concerns to keep funding up in their schools. Well, I must remind him of one thing: colleges were established to teach academics and to educate students who are there to earn degrees. The report suggested colleges raise credit requirements and classroom work, citing the theory that college students have too much free time, thus giving them greater opportunities for drinking and partying.

I take the position that if college students left home whole and sound with self-confidence derived from a positive relationship with their fathers, they would not follow in the footsteps of the world system when they get to college.

Father, you cannot depend on society to protect your seed. Society today has a perverted view of right and wrong. A judge recently ruled against censoring a website that made pornography available to children. The judge felt it was more important to protect freedom of speech than the value of youthful innocence. This judge was of the opinion that children deserve such freedoms, even before they are fully developed. Evil and darkness have spread to such levels this judge felt he had a greater obligation to protect the first amendment right. He said he was actually doing the children a favor by ruling for freedom of speech. That judge's decision not only exposes young children to pornographic perversion, but also conditions them to think of pornography as normal, acceptable behavior.

He did say one thing I agree with, though; and that is the parents could put controls on their computers to stop access to such sites.

I have previously stated it is the responsibility of fathers to protect their seed, and it bears out my observation that society is incapable and unwilling to take a stand for the development of godly, well-rounded individuals.

Fathers, you are the filter of your children's souls. You should be informed about the types of video games your children are using, the websites they have access to, and the music they are listening to.

Researchers have found that teens that listen to certain types of music were more prone to get involved in the type of behaviors expressed in the lyrics of that music.

Fathers, are you too busy to view, or do you even know if your child has a *MySpace* website? You may be in for a shock if you have not been an effective escort. I do not think it is wise to allow children to have so-called "privacy." I have actually heard parents say, "I don't want to have my children think I'm a snoop."

People generally behave themselves when they know someone is watching. When your supervisor is around, you act and conduct yourself in a different manner than when he or she is not around. Or, when you are driving and see that familiar car whose driver has the authority to pull you over and give you a ticket, you check your speed and make sure you come to a complete stop at the next stop sign. When children know there is a loving, caring father who has the authority to pull them over, they will come to complete stops when it comes to right and wrong. They will watch their limits because they know, "My father is watching, and he will pull me over and escort me back to righteousness."

We, as believers, know what pleases the Father; we know he sees our everyday lives and that helps us stay on track. We know Father is watching. That being said, there are some adults who cannot stay on the right course without supervision; should we expect children to stay on course without an escort?

When my seed was living in our house, I had no shame at all checking their backpacks, pants pockets, purses, closets, etc. I was not ashamed to be Columbo, Magnum PI, or Sherlock Holmes. I was going to find out what my seed was doing. I refused to let some television sitcom set a standard for my household. I will not allow the television studios to influence my judgment as to what's best for my household.

Men, when you take a look at fatherhood from God's perspective, you will prayerfully, examine yourself to determine, "Am I ready to be an escort?"

God commanded the children of Israel,

Only take heed to yourself, and diligently keep yourself, lest you forget the things your eyes have seen, and lest they depart from your heart all the days of your life. And teach them to your children and your grandchildren.

Deuteronomy 4:9, NKJV

Father, you are your children's gatekeeper. You have the assignment to bring God into the lives of your seed. Fathers, you first have an experience with God, and you pass that on to your seed, who will in turn pass it on to the next generation for a godly heritage.

Men, your role is so vital that grandchildren who are yet to be conceived will have a good future and a hope because you knew there is no substitute for a father.

Men, when you count the cost of fatherhood, you will find out there is more involved in developing seed than just sowing it. As stated earlier, fatherhood is going to cost you emotionally, financially, and spiritually. Are you prepared to pay that price? When you become a father, you are committing your life to your children and not just for the eighteen to twenty-one years that society dictates. A person is not ready to face all that life has to bring just because they reach the magical age of eighteen or twenty-one.

I have had men tell me, "When my child is eighteen years old, I will be finished with my responsibility to him." That is not the statement of an escort. A father knows his seed may need to draw from its roots, and you will be available to give what is needed for your seed's continual healthy growth and development. I would like to repeat the analogy that we are like God to our children. God refers to himself as "the Potter," and to believers as clay in the hands of the Potter. God molds and shapes us into what will be pleasing to him according to our call and purpose on earth. Fathers, your child is clay in your hands; he can be made whole in your loving hands, or he can develop lumps and leaks without your influence. A child without a father is an unfinished vessel incapable of achieving his intended purpose and discovering his intended destiny.

When I look at people in society today and see the emotional leaks in their lives, I don't blame society, and I don't blame the school systems. I know I'm seeing a person who experienced life without the father.

Let's go back to the beginning to further solidify the father's position in the household. The Bible tells us in Genesis,

> Then the Lord God took the man and put him in the Garden of Eden to tend it and keep it.
>
> Genesis 2:15, NKJV

Notice that a male was the first homemaker. It is not my intent to sound sexist or to attempt to place men above women. I simply want to be on track with God's order. Men and women are both in the category of mankind.

Women are the *female* version of mankind. Males and females are equal in terms of value and worth; our roles and functions are just different.

When God commanded the man Adam to tend and keep the garden, he was telling Adam to cultivate the garden; to protect the garden and to keep it from all intruders. Furthermore, God wanted Adam to put a hedge around the garden and exercise dominion and authority over it. The Garden of Eden was Adam's home. Father, your home is your garden. We know a garden is a place where seeds grow into plants. Men, you are to protect your garden from all intruders; not just the burglar who would try to steal your property, but also the burglars in society who would try and steal your connection to your seed. Spending excessive time on your job or a favorite hobby can be "burglars"; society and the government can be "burglars," all trying to steal God from your children. Society would tell you, "Let your children make their own choices about God." No, I am the keeper of this garden. I am the one who has dominion and authority, and I will exercise the Word of God in this garden.

A godly father knows the only hedge of protection in the earth realm for his seed is himself. We can look all around in our communities and see one unkempt garden after another. Our prisons are filled with people from unkempt gardens. Teachers in our schools have to deal with and face countless children whose lives have gone unprotected and untended by its gardener.

One of the main reasons teachers in the schools cannot teach effectively is because children show up with absolutely no respect or regard for authority. Fathers are the ones first anointed to be under God's authority. They in turn, pass the reverence for authority on to their children by precept and example. Instead of learning institutions, our schools have become behavioral counseling centers to many children from unkempt gardens without escorts. We know what happened in the Garden when Adam did not follow God's instructions. His world was never the same. He went from living in paradise to "toiling and sweating out a living" as the Bible puts it in Genesis 3:19.

I've said it before; we cannot predict the specific area of a child's life that will be affected if the father does not escort his child properly to God.

Adam's boy, Cain, was the first murderer. Adam, Cain's escort and father, killed his relationship with his Father, God. And his seed Cain reproduced after its own kind.

A Godly Heritage

When an escort takes the proper stand for his seed and confesses the appropriate destiny over their lives along with a godly lifestyle, he will see the godly, intended life come to pass for his seed.

When our children were in elementary school, a great influx of people from the Los Angeles vicinity, seeking refuge from the growing gang violence in that area, relocated to our city. Not long after this, several newspaper articles began appearing in our local newspaper, reporting gang-style bank robberies in our small city of Rialto, California. The police attributed the rising problem to people from the city trying to escape the turmoil and unrest by moving to smaller communities.

The problem was not the city, but the people who made up the city. Our church motto is "Change a people and you will change a city." The schools started clamping down and enforcing a stricter dress code, so as to deter possible gang activity. I recall being involved in a neighborhood discussion with other concerned parents. Florence and I continued the conversation at home. She said, "I hope Anthony doesn't join a gang. You never know how your children are going to turn out." I protested that assessment of my son's future being that uncertain. I spoke up. "Yes I do; my son will *never* join a gang." I made the right confession over my seed and took appropriate action to guard his destiny. When I made this confession, I was not yet a Christian. I did not know these Scriptures found in Proverbs were in the Bible.

> You are snared by the words of your mouth; you
> are taken by the words of your mouth.
> Proverbs 6:2, NKJV

> Death and life are in the power of the tongue, and
> those who love it will eat its fruit.
>
> Proverbs 18:21, NKJV

What I did know, by the grace of God, was my son would not end up a statistic. I was determined to escort him around the pitfall of gangs. Principles work with or without your knowledge. You continue to speak faith-filled promises from the Word of God over your seed.

One Saturday, Anthony asked if he could attend a neighborhood boy's birthday party. At the time he was in junior high school, in the eighth grade, I believe. As believers, we did not smother our children and deprive them of normal social interaction. However, like I mentioned earlier, things like boyfriend/girlfriend relationships while they were teens were not allowed.

As a responsible escort, and not a lazy, unconcerned

sperm donor, I asked if the boy's parents were going to be there. Anthony replied, "Yes, I think so." I walked around the corner and had a talk with the boy's father. He assured me he was going to be there to supervise the activity. Later that evening, while Anthony was at the party, I felt led by the Holy Spirit to drive around the block and observe the activities. I was shocked to see Anthony with a group of boys standing in front of the birthday house with their pants sagging and their underwear clearly visible. I kept driving; they did not notice me. I went home, parked the car, and walked around the block. I approached the group of boys, tapped my seed on the shoulder, and said, "Let's go home." Using the most serious pater voice, I reiterated to Anthony our rule of not wearing your pants below your butt and displaying your underwear. "Oh dad," he said, "we all just did that for fun. We don't wear our pants like that all the time!" Unfortunately for him, he did it at the *wrong* time, a time when his escort would see it and not approve. I told my son he disobeyed me and that this qualified for a whipping. He was already a pre-teen in junior high school, and I took him home and whipped him, because I loved him. When you put in the proper time and commitment with your children, whippings will be like holidays. They don't come about that often. I was confirming my stand that he would not be associated with gang activity. Now that was the last time I whipped Anthony. I never saw him with his pants sagging again. His other minor acts of disobedience were easily handled through discussion or restriction.

Fathers, you are so essential that you determine the sex and very blood type of your seed. You are the life of your seed; you are the root of their heritage. The word, *heritage* means to transmit or pass something down to the offspring. Fathers, you are to transmit love, a personal commitment, and a relationship with God down to your seed. Pass on the things of God to your offspring. Let's dissect the word *offspring*. The word, *off* means *divergent, ahead or behind, apart from;* but it also has the meaning of *approaching, coming, or returning. Spring* means to *display motion or action.*

Your child will either live ahead of what you have done (actions); behind what you have done, or apart from what you have done. They can approach what you have done and come into the life you have produced, or they can return to the life you have lived. Offspring will generally live life according to what has been passed down to them emotionally and spiritually in their value system and beliefs, based on life experiences.

Years ago, two teenage brothers who had been charged with burglary were placed in my treatment facility. In group session, we had a difficult time adjusting their belief system that burglarizing businesses was not only unacceptable behavior, but also illegal. These brothers would take a stand, dig in their heels, grit their teeth, and adamantly declare, "There is nothing wrong with stealing as long as you don't get caught. That's what our mother taught us." Their mother had transmitted and passed down to them the value that burglary was okay because businesses had insurance to cover their losses. This was their heritage. Both of those brothers eventually served time in prison as adults. They returned to the heritage that was passed down to them. These two young men grew up disconnected from their father. Their father was a childhood friend of mine, and he also served time in prison.

During my career in corrections, I would often see the pattern of a father and son combination serving time in prison; they usually came from a heritage with a background where a grandfather had also been in prison.

We can see the same type of example in the Bible with reference to the greatest king of all time, David. He had a problem with infidelity. David committed adultery and his son, Solomon, was consumed with the same lust for women. Solomon, like so many other men, followed the heritage of his father's sin.

Now, God told mankind to be fruitful and multiply, but God's intent surely was not for godlessness to be multiplied, but rather, for godliness to be multiplied.

Fathers, that's the reason you are to escort your children into the things of God and not the values of society. Society has lost or cast aside most of its moral values, which is why sin is so prevalent in America.

When God said to be fruitful, he did not mean to make as many babies as you can and forget about the heritage you will pass down to them.

> Then the Lord saw that the wickedness of man was great in the earth, and that every intent of the thoughts of his heart was only evil continually. And the Lord was sorry that he had made man on the earth and he was grieved in his heart.
>
> Genesis 6:5–6, NKJV

God was grieved in his heart because evil was not the heritage he wanted to be passed on. So, God looked and found Noah, a just man; or in other words, a man who wanted just what God wanted: righteousness. God had an assignment for Noah, a father, and his seed, Shem, Ham, and Japheth. Noah wanted to please

God, so he did according to all that God commanded him (Genesis 6:22). As a result, God made supernatural provisions for Noah and his family.

Men, when you purpose in your heart to have a godly heritage, God will provide for your family supernaturally. While the rest of the world is dying in the *flood* of teen pregnancy, alcoholism, drug addiction, and teen suicide, your heritage will be living in the *ark* of righteousness you have *built* for them. Others will perish as they try to navigate the streams of life, but your godly heritage will float high above the circumstances.

And fathers, if you don't correct your children as you escort them, you leave them open for destruction. In I Samuel 2:12, we find an example of a father who knows God, but would not require righteousness from his seed. The Bible says, "the sons of Eli were corrupt." The Message Remix Bible translation of the same Scripture puts it this way, "Eli's own sons were a bad lot." They didn't know God, and could have cared less about the customs of the priests among the people. The literal translation means they were *sons of Belial*, which means they chose to serve the devil.

Christians should pass down a godly heritage in their homes as they are living godly. What a tragedy it is to shout and praise God in church and go home and mistreat your husband or wife. Your seed sees this contradiction in behavior and manner of living. Or, some parents will attend church, but do not require their seed to approach this same type of lifestyle.

I have some relatives whose father regularly attended church and was very active in his church, but he neither required nor escorted his seed into the things of God. Church attendance, for him, was that of social status, not lived out at home. Predictably, his seed have experienced a great deal of destruction in their lives: drug addiction, alcoholism, children out of wedlock, and even early death.

Eli's sons did not just wake up one morning being evil and dishonest. Eli was the fifteenth judge and seventh high priest of Israel. Eli should have produced a godly heritage. Perhaps Eli was too consumed with his call to properly escort his seed.

Get this, men. You fathers may be living in the home with your seed. Perhaps you didn't physically abandon them, but you abandoned them emotionally.

The father of my relatives did not leave his family physically, but he was detached from them emotionally. My relatives said they could not remember spending any significant quality time with their father. He was like the invisible man.

Eli must not have taken his sons' godly heritage seriously. The Bible tells us the boys violated the law and took things that did not belong to them. When the men tried to get Eli's sons to follow the law, they responded by saying,

> Give me the sacrificial offering, or I will take it by force
>
> 1 Samuel 2:16

The Bible says,

> Therefore the sin of the young men was very great before the Lord, for men abhorred the offering of the Lord.
>
> Samuel 2:17, NKJV

The people despised what was going on in the church because of what the man of God's children were doing.

Eli knew what was going on with his sons; this was nothing new. Eli did not put the proper time in to escort these boys into righteousness. Eli tells his boys,

> I've heard everything you've done to Israel and how you 'lay' with the women who assembled at the door of the tabernacle of meeting (church)."
>
> 1 Samuel 2:22, NKJV

Fathers, if you find your seed in sin, deal with the sin; do something about it. Eli did not like what his sons were doing; he should have intervened earlier in their lives before the sin had been "practiced" to the point it became a habit. The biblical principle is if fathers correct or chasten their sons, they will pay them respect (Hebrews 12:9).

Fathers, you are anointed to correct your children. Don't allow society to set the standards in your godly household. The Bible says if you spare the rod, you will spoil them. When something is spoiled, it is not fit for use. Spoiled, untrained, and undisciplined children will not produce the correct heritage. The Bible says if you don't spank them, you don't love them. The Message Remix translation makes the point even clearer.

> A refusal to correct is a refusal to love; love your children by disciplining them.
>
> Proverbs 13:24, Message Remix

We spanked our children as a last resort because we loved them. We find Eli asking his boys,

> Why do you do such things? For, I hear of your evil dealings from all the people.
>
> 1 Samuel 2:23, NKJ

Eli knew why. They were not properly trained at home. Eli is now pleading with his sons,

> It is not a good report that I hear. You make the Lord's people transgress.
>
> 1 Samuel 2:24, NKJV

Christian fathers, if you don't produce godly children, others in the church won't have an example to follow. They will be subject to transgress because of the product you placed in the Body of Christ.

> Nevertheless, they did not heed the voice of their father …
>
> 1 Samuel 2:25, NKJV

Take the example of Anthony and the pants sagging incident. He did something we told him not to do. I don't want to give you the mistaken impression that if you escort your seed, they won't mess up or make mistakes in life. But as you can see, I did not ignore Anthony's disobedience. I was not afraid to confront him. We had a connection; he received love from me on a day-to-day basis. That gave me the legal and emotional right to correct him. Your children may have a godly escort, but they are also in a flesh and blood body. And we know "no good thing dwells in the flesh" nature of mankind. When I worked with violent, felony-committing gang members, I treated them with love and respect. I made them follow the proper rules, but if they stepped out of line, I would "get in their face." They were not my children, so I had no legal right to whip them. But because they knew I did genuinely care about them, they never challenged my right to correct them.

> Foolishness is bound up in the heart of a child; the rod of correction will drive it far from him.
>
> Proverbs 22:15, NKJV

I really love the Message Remix translation of this verse:

> Young people are prone to foolishness and fads; the cure comes through tough-minded discipline.
>
> Proverbs 22:15, Message Remix

Eli should have instituted some tough-minded discipline to cure his sons' foolishness.

Fathers, you must institute a tough-minded approach with your seed, otherwise they will grow up and sprout foolishness in their lives. Teach your godly heritage there is a God to fear (reverence).

> In the fear of the Lord there is strong confidence, *(or we could say tough minds)* and his children have a place of refuge.
>
> Proverbs 14:26, NKJV

Fathers, without your influence in the life of your seed, there is no refuge for them. There is no safe place without you. Growing up without my pater, I felt unsure and never safe. There was no refuge for me as a child. I had no escort.

Disciplining and spanking your children will not kill them; it just sounds like it. It won't damage them emotionally. On the other hand, if you don't discipline or spank them, destruction, in some form or another, will find its way in their lives.

The Word of God admonishes children to,

> Hear, my children, the instruction of a father and give attention to know understanding. My son, give attention to my words; let them not depart from your eyes; for they are life to those who find them.
>
> Proverbs 4:1, 20–22, NKJV

Verse 23 says,

> Keep your heart with all diligence for out of it spring the issues of life.
>
> Proverbs 4:23, NKJV

Fathers, you must be involved and present in your children's lives to teach them about God, since what you pass down to them will eventually spring out of their hearts (spirits). If it is a leaky, broken heart because of a missing escort, your seed will suffer; you will suffer; the kingdom of God will suffer; and society will suffer.

The Bible teaches that a foolish son is the ruin of his father [Proverbs 19:13].

Again, the Message Remix really seals it this way,

> A parent is worn to a frazzle by a stupid child.
>
> Proverbs 19:13, Message Remix

There were six children in my family. Our escort left us unattended and we grew up "stupid." We were *stupid* to righteousness; *stupid* to stability; *stupid* to peace (wholeness; nothing missing and nothing broken); *stupid* to good judgment concerning the issues of life.

We had no escort; no strength-giver to protect, nourish, and guide us. Our search for wholeness led us on various courses of drug addiction, teenage sex, children born out of wedlock, prison terms, living in the streets, and homelessness. We were six broken hearts with emotional leaks everywhere.

The Bible tells fathers to "chasten your son while there is hope and do not set your heart on his destruction." And, if that's not clear enough for you, let's read the Message Remix translation of Proverbs 19:18,

> Discipline your children while you still have the chance; indulging them destroys them.
>
> Proverbs 19:18, Message Remix

I don't want you to get the notion that I'm bashing my dad. I'm not. That was never my intent. I'm simply building a foundation and making the case for those men who have not yet made the fatal mistake of not escorting their seed. This truth is evident in the fact that fathers are missing in 70% of homes in the black community today.

Men, we need to escort our godly children into

America and save them from the foolishness all around them.

> A foolish son is a grief to his father and bitterness to her who bore him.

Proverbs 17:25, NKJV

The Message Remix translation says it like this,

> A surly, stupid child is sheer pain to a father, a bitter pill for a mother to swallow."

Proverbs 17:25, Message Remix

I have counseled so many parents who did not put the proper godly foundation into their children, and it became painful to live with these children. The parents had a difficult time swallowing the lifestyles their children had fallen into.

Eli was about to experience what Proverbs 19:18 talks about. He did not discipline his sons when he had the chance. Fathers, if you don't discipline your children, society or Satan will discipline them, and there will be no love in it, just punishment. God sent a message to Eli, and it was not good news. Let's pick it up in 1 Samuel:

> Then a man of God came to Eli and said to him, 'thus says the Lord: Did I not clearly reveal myself to the house of your father when they were in Egypt in Pharaoh's house? Did I not choose him out of all the tribes of Israel to be my priest, to offer upon my altar, to burn incense, and to wear an ephod before me? And did I not give to the house of your father all the offerings of the chil-

dren of Israel made by fire? Why do you kick at my sacrifice and my offering which I have commanded in my dwelling place, and honor your sons more than me?'"

1 Samuel 2:27–29, NKJV

God was telling Eli, "You did not follow my instructions in escorting your children." Notice God is taking Eli's sons' transgressions personally.

Now in contextual teaching, God took it personally because of Eli's position as high priest; the sin was against God himself. Eli's sons' had no messiah to intercede for them (I Samuel 2:25), and destruction would be their penalty.

I have personally observed Christian parents cosign the sin behavior of their children. I have observed born again, spirit-filled believers accept a lifestyle of sin from their children. Florence and I taught our children that we would love them no matter what they did. However, we also let them know we would not support them in any form of disobedience. If my children had decided to "shack up" with someone, we would not visit them at the residence. If they robbed God and did not tithe, we would not give them any financial assistance. If they engaged in drugs or drinking, their behavior would not be tolerated in our presence.

Our stand against sin had nothing to do with our love for them, but everything to do with our love for God. Our children knew we would never put them before God. We need God in our lives and in our affairs. We need his mercy and grace at work every day of our lives. We needed God's protection and provisions. I wanted my seed to see the reality of obeying God and

116 DR. CLYDE A. STEWART

the consequences of disobeying him. I was determined to build a godly heritage so that my children's children could be blessed because they had an escort and they experienced life with a father.

King David had a godly escort, Jesse. When God sent the prophet Samuel on assignment, he instructed the prophet,

> Fill thine horn with oil, and go, I will send thee to Jesse the Bethlehemite: for I have provided me a king among his sons.
>
> 1 Samuel 16:1, KJV

There is no mention of David's mother. We can say Jesse was a godly man because when Samuel said,

> Sanctify yourselves, and come let's make a sacrifice to the Lord with your sons.
>
> I Samuel 16:5, NKJV

Jesse knew what Samuel was referring to and he agreed to worship God.

> And Saul said unto his servants, provide me now a man that can play well, and bring him to me. Then answered one of the servants, and said, 'Behold, I have seen a son of Jesse the Bethlehemite, that is cunning in playing, and a mighty valiant man, and a man of war, and prudent in matters, and a comely person, and the Lord is with him.'
>
> 1 Samuel 16:17–18, KJV

Clearly the Lord was with David. Jesse had done such an excellent job escorting David that his reputation reached the king's court. David was so stable he was fit to be in the presence of royalty. Wow, what a resume! Because of his pater Jesse, David had an invite to the king's palace. David had rhythm; he was a skillful musician; he was smart, well-mannered, courageous, and fit to be in the presence of the greatest man in the land.

When you're at the malls, grocery store, or schools, and you see the behavior and the language of some children, you would not want to take them to a circus, let alone take them around a king or president. So many of them are untrained, unloved, and like wild weeds growing in society today. It's not uncommon these days to see children out in public with their underwear exposed, even wearing pajamas and bedroom slippers. In this condition they could never make it to the palaces of life.

Godly fathers can train their seed to be fit for the high places in life, instead of the jails and crack houses of society. Men, if you develop a godly heritage for your children, people will see God is with them, and it will open doors to your seed than no man can close. God said David was a man after his own heart. I want my seed to be after God's heart, not the world's heart. The Bible says David danced before the Lord with all his might. I'd rather have my seed dance before the Lord with all their heart instead of shaking their rumps in a music video or at a club until two o'clock in the morning, as I did before I knew any better.

Now remember this: David was not a perfect man just because he had an escort. He made mistakes, too, but he was able to overcome them.

King Saul sent word to Jesse, "Send your son David to me, the one who tends sheep." The king immediately took a liking to David and appointed him to be his right hand man. Like David, your child may be in the background or out in the field; but if they have a heart for God, they will experience a royal life too.

> Saul sent word back to Jesse, 'Thank you. David will stay here. He's just the one I was looking for. I'm very impressed by him.'
>
> 1 Samuel 16:22, Message Remix

How does your seed affect its surroundings? Whether they're at school or out in the workforce, are others so impressed with them that they would make the statement, "This is just the type of person I was looking to promote"?

Or, because your seed was unloved, do they now openly display emotional leaks and dysfunctional behavior to the point that people shun them or are disgusted at the very thought of interacting with them?

Let's take a look at a New Testament example of a young man who was brought up with a godly heritage.

> Now behold, one came and said to Him, 'Good Teacher, what good thing shall I do that I may have eternal life?'
>
> Matthew 19:16, NKJV

Jesus then gave the young man a list of things that godly people do. It's quite amazing that a young man had a heart for godliness and not foolishness. Jesus told the young man what to do and the he responded by saying, "I have done all these things since I was a boy." That's an indication to me this young man had a father and a godly heritage established in his life. Jesus found one "leak" in the young man's life: the love of money. Jesus did not find fault with the young man for being rich; his chief concern was that he was not willing to obey. The Bible says he went away sorrowful, for he had great possessions. The young man had acquired riches in the first place because of his godly heritage and his obedience to God from the time he was a boy. We read in Proverbs 10:22 NKJ, "the blessing of the Lord makes one rich, and He adds no sorrow with it."

If God was against people being rich, why would he bless them financially to begin with? When you put God first and he tells you to give, there should be no sorrow attached to your giving. Since you know he's the one who made you rich in the first place, you have no problem letting go of whatever he tells you.

This rich young ruler had a problem with the "let go." Jesus told him to sell what he had and to give to the poor. When you sell something you generally get a profit or, at the very least, break even. Jesus then told him to give to the poor. The Bible says when you give to the poor, you are lending to the Lord. And no one pays dividends like the Lord. The biblical principle in Luke 6:38 (NKJV) is, "give and it shall be given back to you; good measure, pressed down, shaken together and running over shall men give back to your bosom." Jesus was actually trying to get the young man to trust in him and not his possessions. If the young man had only listened to Jesus, he would have received more than what he started with. Jesus knows how to handle finances. He had a staff of twelve disciples himself, and they all lived on Jesus' ability to provide for them.

Teach your godly heritage to depend on God to show them how to live a good life. I escorted my seed into being tithers and givers. Whenever they received allowances, birthday money, Christmas money, they were taught to tithe from their increase. Always bring God an offering when you come into the house of the Lord. They are never too young to be introduced to the things of God if you want to establish a godly heritage in them.

One account in the Bible tells how escorts brought their children to Jesus one day, hoping he would lay hands on them and pray over them.

> The disciples shooed them off. But Jesus intervened: "Let the children alone, don't prevent them from coming to me. God's kingdom is made up of people like these."
>
> Matthew 19:13–14, Message Remix

I tell you, fathers, Jesus doesn't take it lightly when little ones are abused and hurt. Here's what else he says about it. "If you cause one of the little ones to stumble and fall, it is better if you were never born, or that you would tie a boulder around your neck and jump into the sea." Sounds like Jesus was ticked off, doesn't it? When it comes to children, Jesus will intervene.

Fathers, your children are never too young to be presented to the Lord. We conduct baby dedications at our church. We don't baptize babies; that will come later when they are old enough to understand and accept the Lord Jesus.

Baby dedications are a commitment that begins with a confession of faith by loving parents. The parents are making a commitment to God and the world that this child will not serve sin as a lifestyle, thus committing the child to a godly heritage.

I regularly have the opportunity to observe the destruction in people's lives because of no God and no escort. Even as I'm writing this book, a newspaper article on my desk momentarily grabs my attention. A twenty-six-year-old black man has been convicted of killing a twenty-seven-year-old black man over gang violence. Pure nonsense! One man's life is gone; and the other is sentenced to life in prison without parole. The destinies of these two men now destroyed; the potential they once possessed can never come to pass.

I then read about two teenage boys in custody for the apparent gang-related shooting death of a fifteen-year-old boy, killed as he played basketball. Incidents like this are occurring so routinely they have become accepted by society. Not *condoned*, but accepted. We are so conditioned that stories like this don't even shock us anymore. These two deaths and the wasted lives in prison would have never taken place if these boys had a godly heritage and an escort to give them strength and nourishment. I can safely hypothesize these boys did not have a pater or a foundation of righteousness established in their lives.

Here is another account that saddens me. Two young men robbed a hair salon at gunpoint. They robbed all the patrons. When they discovered one of the customers was an off-duty police officer, the boys shot and killed him. Next they robbed a pizza parlor. Shortly thereafter, they were apprehended and arrested carrying the gun and a total of $211.00. Those unescorted young men will spend their lives in prison because of a life of unrighteousness; not to mention the loss of a police officer's life and the effect his death will have on his family. When children grow up with emotional leaks, all of society suffers. We are influenced by a fast-paced "spirit" operating in society: High speed Internet, fast food, fast money, and fast fame (*Who Wants to Be a Millionaire?*, *America's Next Top Model*, *American Idol*). After just a few weeks or months, society attempts to have our children think life is fast and easy. So children grow up fast, without the discipline, maturity, or patience to live balanced lives.

Parents are placing their children in front of the television, video games, and computers for hours. Day care centers are escorting children instead of parents. There are several middle school teachers in our congregation; all report the increase in sexual activity among pre-teens. Parents are afraid to spank their children, or to even act in their best interest. I can recall our son being upset with us because we drove 56 miles one way to church. Sitting in the back seat of the car, he complained, "I don't see why we have to drive all this way just to go to church." Well, he was only eleven years old; I would not expect an eleven-year-old to have much insight about anything. I was his escort; I have his best interests at heart. My goal was to develop a godly heritage in my house. I explained, "Anthony, people drive this far five days a week to go to work. When it comes to God, no effort is too great." He still protested, "I don't like it. I'm mad." I calmly told him he could be mad if he chose to be.

I was in full escort mode when I told him, "Anthony, you can go to church mad; or you can go glad, but you're going." I explained to him that I was responsible to

God to deposit godly experiences in his life and regular church attendance is necessary for spiritual development. I said, "God gives us permission to be angry, but he tells us not to let the sun go down holding on to the anger." By the time we drove home and had eaten lunch, his anger was gone.

Men, when you love your children and escort them, they will be capable of following your orders without rebelling. I strongly disagree with the cliché, *I grew up in the church.* Children do not grow up in church! Children may attend church as they are growing but children *grow up* at home. Fathers, if godliness is your consistent everyday lifestyle, you will produce godly adults. Children play, bathe, eat, and sleep at home. They attend church two or three days a week for a couple of hours. Six hours a week of mere church attendance will not impact their lives. It's the bulk of the other hours that transpire in their lives that count. Fathers, if you will live godly before your children and not just preach to them, they will see God is real. Charmaine and Anthony learned from what I said, but they learned to believe by what I did. When you are able to make God real to your seed, he will not be just a "church" God, but a God for life.

When I began pastoring Westside Christian Center, my son was twenty-one years old; a grown man by society's standards. My daily escorting duties were over for Anthony; however, I was still his life escort. I did not tell him he had to attend our church. He was now old enough to choose what would keep him in a godly heritage. He came to me and said, "Dad, the Lord spoke to my heart about something." I asked, "Really?" He said, "Yes. There are several girls that I take to the movies, dinner, etc., but I don't think I should be dating so freely and so many different people." He went on to say, "I don't think it gives the right impression, with you being a pastor." I guess Anthony felt the conviction for being a Christian "Mack Daddy." I said, "Wow. That's wonderful; sounds like godly wisdom to me. I sure do appreciate your concern to avoid the 'appearance of evil.'" I had no idea how many girls Anthony was dating, but God knew. Fathers, when you make it your priority to establish a godly heritage in your life, Almighty God makes it a priority to help you fulfill your goal.

Years later, when my son interviewed for a particular profession, the company interviewer could not believe that he had never been arrested. I'm not talking about being convicted of a crime, but never *arrested*. He was just as amazed to learn Anthony never used illegal drugs, even "recreationally," as they put it. The interviewer cautioned him, "We do an extensive background check. If we find any discrepancies, it will disqualify you. Are you sure you're telling us the truth?" As a black man in traditional American society and reading between the lines, I know what the interviewer was insinuating. *How in the world could it be that a twenty-four-year-old black man has never been arrested or used drugs? That's impossible.*

Well, without the godly escort experience, I, too, would find it difficult to believe. I grew up in the "hood," where poverty, arrests, teen pregnancy, single parent households, drug addiction, violence, and prison were a commonplace experience for me.

I had a revelation from God early on. I would confess as a young boy, "When I grow up, I am never going to leave my wife and family. My children will never be poor or sad." Little did I know then, God was depositing a godly heritage in my heart. When I started working in prisons and juvenile facilities, I saw firsthand what the experience of *life without the father* did to boys and men. We know the world's system is not fair. The Bible says that Satan is the god of this world. I would see African American and Hispanic males receive harsher punishments and longer sentences for the same crimes committed by white offenders. It was not difficult to see the injustices Satan worked through the court systems. There was no way my seed would ever be at the mercy of a system that was influenced by darkness. When God called me out of darkness (sin), he called my seed out of darkness. It was the will of God to have righteousness established in the Stewart family. But, as the vessel through which God would work to accomplish this, I had the responsibility to carry it out. I wanted to build godly character and consciousness in my seed. Your children may have talents and gifts that may make their lives better; please don't send them out into the world without godly character. Gifts and talents may take them to high places, and with godly character, they will be able to maintain their position in those places.

Fathers, we will make our mark in the earth realm by influencing our seed with godliness. As a result of being your seed's escort, they are anointed for a godly heritage. In my research, I discovered when a man and woman have sexual intercourse (*married* men and women), some three and one-half million sperm are released by the male. In some rare cases, twins, triplets, quadruplets, etc. are conceived. But generally speaking, the overwhelming majority of women give birth to one baby at a time. I'm sure you're familiar with the term, "one in a million." Well, fathers, your child is one in three and one-half million! Out of three and one-half million chances to fertilize your wife's egg, the child who is now under your influence was specially chosen and is here for a godly reason. He or she is not an accident, but a divine accomplishment to be handled with godly care. Fathers, there are various accounts in Scripture where men of God give credit to God for the children in their lives. Fathers, look at your seed as you would a wise, well thought-out investment. After all, you will spend hundreds of thousands of dollars in raising your child: educating them; feeding and clothing them; paying for their medical expenses; buying their toys; funding recreational activities. Then there is your investment of time, sweat, tears, and prayers, all well worth the effort it takes to produce spiritually whole, emotionally sound, and physically healthy adults.

I remember the dental bills for Anthony's and Charmaine's braces: $3,000 each! Some $6,000 to insure they would go through life with straight teeth and beautiful smiles. How foolish it would have been for me to go to the expense and time of taking them to numerous dental appointments for them to have straight teeth, just to have them grow up and live a crooked life without God. I protected my godly investment. I didn't want my daughter, or son for that matter, to choose an ungodly mate who could possibly physically abuse them and knock out the $6,000 teeth I paid for. I made an investment in them, and I endeavored to escort them to safety.

Fathers, with today's technology it is difficult, if not

impossible, for you to shirk your financial responsibility to your seed. You may skip out on your responsibility to physically escort your seed, but the District Attorney's office in your county has ways of making sure you stand up to your financial responsibility. District Attorney's offices have gotten creative in getting you to step up and be a financially responsible man. I have talked to men who have suffered the loss of their driver's licenses, professional licenses, and their freedom for not escorting their seed financially. By the way, it's futile trying to disown your seed; DNA will lead the authorities straight to the one who sowed the seed. Men, the ability to make a baby does not qualify you as an escort. Having the *heart* of a father not only qualifies you, but then demands you escort your seed.

A few moments of sexual gratification are not worth the expense of inflicting years of excruciating emotional pain on a child or your wallet. Excuses and sorry explanations will not exempt you from the expectation that you were to escort your seed. Society won't accept your excuses, and neither will God. You see, your children are a gift from God. In Genesis, we see the resolution of a family feud between Jacob and Esau.

> But Esau ran to meet him, and embraced him, and fell on his neck and kissed him, and they wept. And, he lifted his eyes and saw the women and children, and said, 'Who are these with you?' So he (Jacob) said, 'The children whom God has graciously given your servant.'
>
> Genesis 33:4–5, NKJV

In Genesis 48, a generation later, we see Jacob (Israel) now an old man, meeting with his son's children.

> Then Israel saw Joseph's sons, and said, 'Who are these?' Joseph said to his father, 'They are my sons, whom God has given me in this place.' And he said, 'Please bring them to me, and I will bless them.'
>
> Genesis 48:8–9 NKJV

We then find Joshua still working God's plan for a godly heritage.

> And Joshua said to all the people, thus says the Lord God of Israel: "Your fathers, including Terah, the father of Abraham and the father of Nahor, dwelt on the other side of the River in old time; and they served other gods. Then I took your father Abraham from the other side of the River, led him throughout all the land of Canaan, and multiplied his descendants and gave him Isaac."
>
> Joshua 24: 2–3, NKJV

Fathers, God needed to get us to the "other side" in order to get us out of sin and darkness. If you stand against the righteousness and holiness of God, you are standing against your seed's future success and wholeness. Abraham had to be willing to trust God and step out of the dysfunction of his family. Fathers, you can be the start of something godly in your family. Everything good or bad has a beginning. Cross on over to the marvelous light. You'll be able to see clearly.

God tells the man Abraham,

Get out of your country, from your family and from your father's house...

Genesis 12:1, NKJV

You would say, "Pastor Stewart, this seems contrary to your whole teaching." Not so fast. Abraham's family was very dysfunctional: a band of idolaters and ungodly worshipers of everything but the Lord. When God commanded Abram to "get out of your country, from your family, out of your father's house," it was not God's plan to break up Abraham's family, but to break down the ungodliness in the family. This was a serious demand, because it required Abram to leave his identity. At the time, people in this region simply did not just pick up and leave. It was unheard of. The country was the region of Abram's dwelling; the family was his clan, and his father's house was where he had natural responsibilities and leadership. Upon the death of his father, Terah, Abram would have become the leader of this dysfunctional bunch. Fathers, spiritual responsibility takes precedence over natural traditions. Spiritual accountability to God will change your family's destiny.

During Abram's time, only the poverty-stricken, the defeated, the landless, and fugitives would wander, move about, and leave their ancestral homes. But the Lord's words to Abram commanded that he was to leave everything and go to a place that God would not even confirm ("a land that I will show you") until Abram got there. Abram had no explainable reason to change his surroundings. Everything looked and sounded good to him.

Fathers, you may have grown up in a place and

around people that seemed right and okay to you, like men making babies and not escorting them to a godly heritage. Perhaps your father did not escort you, or you may have never even met him and you learned about life from other ungodly sources. You are content to stay around your clan; to stay in the cycle of curses that have already caused ruin in your family.

I want you to read this book as coming from the mouth of Almighty God himself. God is intervening in your life. God is invading your space. God is getting in your face. He's saying, "Come with me to a place that I will show you."

Before I left my clan, my country, and my way of thinking, I thought I was a pretty good father. I provided well for my seed; I loved my children; I did not abandon them and leave them to fend for themselves. But, until I presented them to God, I was not the escort that God the Father wanted me to be. You must understand, my children had my sin nature. That was all I had to pass on to them. All my love, all my money, all my care and concern could not save them from sin. Satan had a plan to kill and destroy their lives. My children were living under the curse of the Stewart and Breland families. Our children inherited the nature of my wife and me. In our family tree, like yours, there were a lot of ungodly negative curses. You find a lot of nuts and monkeys in trees, and without Christ, you will raise a child that will grow up and eventually display some nutty primate behavior. There is a biblical escape clause from your family tree. You must be born again. Jesus was teaching a man named Nicodemus this awesome spiritual truth. Nicodemus, looking at it from a natural standpoint, asked Jesus,

How can a man be born when he is old? Can he enter a second time into his mother's womb and be born?

John 3:4, NKJV

Heavens no! What mother would want to go through childbirth a second time and bear the same child? Not to mention, you are now a tad bit over the normal six, seven, or eight-pound limit. Mama would definitely decline.

Jesus answered,

Most assuredly, I say to you, unless one is born of water and the Spirit, he cannot enter the kingdom of God.

John 3:5, NKJV

Fathers, you must escort your seed to Jesus from the moment they are conceived in their mother's womb. Start praying and confessing salvation over your seed immediately. Florence and I confessed our children will never serve sin as a way of life. They would serve God all the days of their lives. They would never use drugs or alcohol; they would not have children out of wedlock. My seed would never wind up begging bread. It is never too early to see your children serving God; but tragically, it can be too late.

Jesus went on to explain to Nicodemus and the world, "That which is born of the flesh is flesh, and that which is born of the Spirit is spirit." When Jesus mentioned being born of water, he was referring to himself, the Word of God. When he mentioned Spirit, he was referring to the Spirit of God, or a spiritual birth. The Word of God tells us,

> Since you have purified your souls in obeying the truth (the Word of God), through the Spirit in sincere love of the brethren, love one another fervently, with a pure heart.
>
> 1 Peter 1:22, NKJV

Only born again people can love each other with a pure heart; with no ulterior motives or hidden agendas—just a sure foundation of a sound person.

> Having been born again, not of corruptible seed but incorruptible, through the Word of God which lives and abides forever.
>
> 1 Peter 1:23, NKJ

The Message Remix explains this born again truth.

> Now that you've cleaned up your lives by following the truth, love one another as if your lives depended on it. Your new life is not like your old life. Your old birth came from mortal sperm; your new birth comes from God's living word. Just think: a life conceived by God himself!
>
> 1 Peter 1:23, Message Remix

That's the life I want to pass down to my seed. The Scripture goes on to say in verse 24, "the glory of man, like flowers and grass, withers." That's all we can pass on to our children; but I can lead them to eternal life. Verse 25, "But the word of the Lord endures forever."

That's the heritage I want to leave or my seed. Not just money, property, and my DNA, but a godly heritage that will last them an eternity. Material things that I may leave them, they too will one day have to leave. But, if I can escort them to Jesus, they can take him every place they go, right into the very presence of God. Proverbs 13:22 says,

> A good man leaves an inheritance to his children's children.
>
> Proverbs 13:22, NKJV

The Living Bible says,

> "When a good man dies, he leaves an inheritance to his grandchildren."
>
> Proverbs 13:22, TLB

And my favorite,

> A good life gets passed on to the grandchildren.
>
> Proverbs 13:22, Message Remix

This Scripture is generally taught to prove that God wants us to live a financially secure and prosperous life while we are on the earth. Well, I like to look deep into the heart and intent of God. I agree God has built material prosperity into his promises, but I believe his primary intent is for us to lead our children's children into a godly inheritance. I truly believe my children could not have stepped into righteousness at an early age without my assistance. It is a waste of life and resources to go through hell for twenty or thirty years and then clean up. There's no benefit in going through two failed marriages, four children and a stint in rehab before you clean up. It is far more productive to start your life out in Christ avoiding the pitfall; and, fathers, you are instrumental in this process. Proverbs 20:7 (NKJV), "the righteous man walks in his integrity; his children are blessed after him." Again, let's get some clarity from the Message Remix. "God-loyal people, living honest lives, make it much easier for their children."

Fathers, why not make it easier on your seed? Life is difficult enough. You have the God-given commission to make life easier on your seed as you escort them to the truth. Fathers, walk your life out in front of your children. Don't have a church life, a home life and yet still, a job or business life. Be consistent for your seed. Be like Jesus: the same yesterday, today, and forever. It will cause your children to be blessed. Fathers, the attributes and values you pass down as vital to a good life will be accepted and lived by your children.

My son and I love sports. Whether high school, college, or professional, we enjoy watching sports on television or going to a good game. But, as much as we both love rousing athletic competition, I did not give my son the impression that sports were more important than God. I mentioned earlier how upset my son would get about our long drive to church each Sunday. My integrity was really put to the test the first time the Super Bowl challenged my stand of putting God first. The big game would be televised about two hours before we got home from church. I told my son, "God and my commitment at church are more important than the Super Bowl."

I was serving as an usher at church; my pastor and my church were counting on me being there. Now, I could have missed church and no one would have questioned me about it. I would not have felt guilty or dirty if I had stayed home and watched the game. God does not put us in religious bondages. *Whom the Son has set free, is free indeed.* Free to stay home and watch football, if you so choose. I was more interested in hearing the Sunday teaching and walking in the integrity of escorting my seed, by example, to put God first. That decision helped my faith to grow and served as proof to me that I was truly a man of integrity in keeping my word. I have read about men being addicted to sports and of wives who threatened to leave their husbands because of neglect; or, husbands being upset for days after "their team" loses a game, throwing things and using profanity in front of their children; some men even had to go to therapy, all for a game that will not benefit his home life.

Men, I challenge you to contact "your team" if your children are out of control, in jail, or on their deathbed. Invite the members of "your team" to your child's graduation or to help you with a doctor's bill. Sports in America are all about money and entertainment. There's nothing wrong with watching them, but are you at least as interested in your child's life as you are in the standing of "your team"? Most men can quote their favorite team's statistics, players, hits, scores, etc. But they do not know their child's grade point average or the character of their children's friends. Remember men, you have "one in three and one-half million" sitting next to you in your home. Do you have the next Dr. Clyde Stewart, Apostle Frederick K. C. Price, Barack

Obama, or Condoleeza Rice in your home? Consider this: you could be influencing the next mayor, senator, or president. Bill Gates is said to be one of the richest men in the world. Is there a Bill Gates in your home, needing an escort to reach his proper destiny?

When your children reach their greatness, they will be successful in the things of God first and then the business world and give the glory to God. If Satan can get a foothold in the life of your seed, his plan is to destroy what could have been.

I remember reading about a tragic incident involving two young girls, one an eight-month-old infant, the other a six-year-old. These children had been locked inside an apartment for four days, as the scorching August temperatures outside reached 108! The article stated the windows were shut and there was no air conditioning. These poor children became severely dehydrated and subsequently died. The investigators reported the mother left home in search of drugs. What a terrible mother. Yes, but where was the escort? These two young girls will never reach their destinies. And their mother was charged with double murder.

When you read of teenage boys shooting one another or carjacking someone, you wonder, *how can children be so angry?* I no longer wonder. I've heard the stories firsthand. I've seen the anger of the unfulfilled and destiny-deprived. Prisons and jails filled with unfulfilled lives, without an escort. How many early deaths have innocent seed suffered because of demonic influence that caused a father to abort his seed? You may think of a mother aborting a developing fetus. Well, there are many men who have committed abortions, *after* the birth, leaving his seed unattended in a sin-sick world. Our children's destiny is our responsibility.

As you can tell, I use real life cases to teach the principal of escort-ship. Here's yet another life, void of a godly heritage, that ended in early death. A mother was charged with and tried for child neglect in the death of her thirteen-year-old daughter who weighed in excess of six hundred pounds. The attorney for the mother argued she was being charged for something she had no control over. Neighbors and family members testified the girl weighed two hundred pounds when she was only seven years old. The Bible tells us to train our children. "Train" is a military term. It means to *make them do it*. There is no way a seven-year-old should be allowed to choose his or her own diet. Men, any of you who have served in the military know the training you had to endure to become a good soldier. They made you rise early; they made you march; they made you dress a certain way; they made you eat foods to give you stamina and strength; all of which was conducive to transforming you into a skilled and disciplined soldier.

The article quoted the girl's mother, saying the child "demanded food" and there was "nothing she could do about it." Family members stated they reported to Child Protective Services their concern over the child's weight years ago, but no action was ever taken. It is not God's plan for Child Protective Services to protect our children. Where was her protector? Where was the escort who "aborted" her? There was no mention of the little girl's escort. God promises, "With long life will I satisfy you and show you my salvation." This promise is connected to a godly heritage. No godly heritage, no promise fulfilled.

Fathers, when you married the mother of your children, you made a covenant with her, "till death do you part." If you depart and leave (you are a covenant breaker), you nullify the promises of God. If you leave children behind, they too, will grow up to be covenant breakers, if they live that long. Protect their godly heritage. Their very lives depend on it.

Do You Know Where My Father Is?

I have mentioned my professional background in corrections several times throughout this book. I worked in three different California penal institutions for a period of six years, then owned and operated three residential treatment facilities for twelve years. The treatment facilities treated over six hundred and fifty juvenile offenders. In addition, I counseled thousands of teen boys and girls in the California foster care system.

I personally escorted two spiritually and emotionally healthy children who are now functional, productive adults in society and the Body of Christ. Keep in mind, because I escorted my children does not mean they are perfect. However, escorting them sealed them against a destructive lifestyle.

With my background in corrections and my expertise as a successful business owner of treatment facilities for juvenile offenders, I was regularly called to testify as an expert witness for defense lawyers or prosecutors. I would take the stand to give my assessment and opinion about the competency of an offender to cope with state prison. I brought up my background to set the scene for the divine revelation I want to share with you.

A former probation officer recently contacted me. He retired and is now working as an investigator for a law firm. He contacted me to ask if I would interview and possibly testify about the competency of one of his clients. I was quite hesitant to accept his proposition, as I had not done such work in several years. I really had no interest in consenting—until the Holy Spirit spoke to my heart and said, "Go. God tells you to go. He wants you to go. If you are a servant, you obey."

This was quite an inconvenience for me; the young man was housed in a county jail that was a ninety-minute drive from my office. Serving God will sometimes be an inconvenience to your schedule, but a necessity to your destiny.

The law firm had my name added to the list of approved visitors, and the following day I headed out to the county jail. Now, this was a new facility that I was not familiar with; as I said, I had been out of the corrections loop for years. I had been given directions by his office, as well as the most up-to-date, computer-assisted traveling instructions. I got to the particular city, but the directions could not get me to my desired destination. Good intentions, inspiration from God, but faulty directions will always delay destiny. I drove around (as men do) for one hour, trying to find this jail. After all, how hard can it be to find a jail? Criminals find their way there all the time. I got frustrated, and finally gave up. I felt justified as I said to myself, "I don't have time for this anyway." I tried to call the probation officer from my cell phone. He was not available. I got back on the freeway, and began planning how I would apologize for not being able to find the jail and bow out of the expert witness business for good.

God still had a bigger reason for me to go to that county jail. I got back to the office and called the former probation officer again. As I shared with him my perplexity in wasting my time and resources trying to find the county jail, he replied, "Oh my, I forgot to change the information for one of the turns. The *new* street is not on the updated Map Quest directions. You needed to turn on (he named the particular street) to get to the jail." How many times have we had our destinies delayed due to taking a wrong turn?

Fathers, if you take a wrong turn, leaving your seed without an escort, he or she will find their destiny delayed, if not destroyed altogether. I knew in my spirit God wanted me to follow through with the assignment. I asked the gentleman to put my name back on the approved visitors list for the next day.

The following day I returned to the city, made the adjustment in directions, and there it was. Driving up to a correctional facility can be intimidating and depressing, which is probably why I didn't want to go. Having worked in this type of demonic environment, I was not excited about going through the process. As a rule, courtesy and customer service is not the jail staff's forte. What they generally see in you is a potential problem; after all, you are here to visit a criminal. Your intentions are thoroughly scrutinized.

However, God's favor was upon me. I had not yet been approved as a new visitor, but the supervisor said to "let the man of God in anyway." I was on kingdom business for the Father. Brother, sister: when you determine to obey God, what you think to be difficult will be made easy because he is ordering your steps.

Without delay, I was escorted to the waiting room. I realized then there was another reason I was reluctant to go to the institution: you can find yourself waiting for hours. Like I said, customer service is not a top concern of the staff. When I got to the waiting room, which was not yet inside the jail itself, there was an elderly lady, a husband and wife, and two single young girls already seated. One of the girls was there by herself, and the other was a young black teenage girl with a little boy.

As I sat there, I thought about the last time I was in the waiting room of a jail. It was approximately five years earlier; I had been summoned to evaluate a former client of mine who had been in my boys' home when he was fourteen years old. I will call him AJ. He is now twenty-one years old and facing the crisis of his life. AJ had never met his escort (father); his mother had turned to a life of drugs, and his grandmother had attempted to escort him through life.

I'll repeat a truth I spoke of earlier: *there is no substitute for a father.* Stepparents, grandparents, uncles, aunts, or the government cannot effectively and efficiently escort another man's seed like he could. If you are a football fan, you may recall a pro bowl receiver who was constantly in the news during the 2005 and 2006 football seasons. He was in one predicament after another and I will never forget his childhood story of how he was raised by his grandmother. He pledged his love to his grandmother for raising him. But if you know the player I'm referring to, this multi-millionaire professional athlete displayed one emotional leak after another. Pro bowl status at the height of his profession, fame, and fortune could not put him back together again. This is society's definition of accomplishment and success; but it could not plug his emotional leaks. He was disconnected from his father. This athlete talked about feeling alone and separated from life as he grew up in his grandmother's house, and how he couldn't bring himself to trust anybody. Things had gotten so bad for him, that it was alleged that he tried to commit suicide by overdosing on prescription medication. Only a relationship with a loving heavenly Father can save this man.

I first met AJ when he was fourteen years old, disconnected from his father, in Juvenile Hall, and facing multiple felony charges. He was placed in my custody. He was angry and repeatedly displayed violent behavior and aggression toward others. This young boy was in emotional pain with a ten-story defensive wall built around him to protect him from further emotional pain. He was not going to let anyone else ever hurt him again. AJ joined a neighborhood street gang and he was on a path of destruction that would culminate on his twenty-first birthday.

The Scripture in Colossians speaks specifically to fathers:

> Fathers, do not embitter your children, or they will become discouraged.
>
> Colossians 3:21, NIV

AJ was both *bitter* and *discouraged* when he came to my program. He lived there for two years. We loved him, treated him with counseling, enrolled him in school, made him dress properly, and watched over his life.

But Stewart's Home for Boys was no substitute for his father. AJ left my program, went back to the gangs, began selling drugs, and eventually killed another young man during a drug deal. I was asked to interview him and testify on his behalf as to the type of life he had faced as a child. I was heartbroken when I later learned AJ was sentenced to the death penalty days before his twenty-first birthday. His whole life was wasted; this was a real life tragedy that took twenty years and eleven months to harvest. This seed was sown in the earth realm and was never developed or nourished. AJ destroyed his life and the life of the man he killed. AJ's family suffers; the victim's family suffers; society suffers; all because this young man had a life without the father.

My thoughts turn back to my upcoming interview with this nineteen-year-old, who is facing prison on an armed robbery charge. He had never been arrested before, but no doubt was without a godly escort. If you recall, I described the people in the waiting room with me, there to visit other inmates. One was a young black teenage girl who had a little boy about four or five years old with her. The waiting room was adjacent to the jail visiting room. A sheriff's deputy stood guard between a big, heavy screen door and the door to the visiting room. He would activate a buzzer to allow authorized personnel to enter or exit.

A sheriff's deputy would approach the door, then

you could hear this loud buzz, a thump when the door opened, and a deep reverberating slam as the door closed shut.

The first deputy came up to the door; as the guard let him in, the loud buzz caused me to look up. I saw the deputy push open the door with a thump, and then it slammed shut. As the deputy entered our waiting room, the little boy jumped out of his seat, ran up to the deputy, and shouted with genuine and utmost sincerity, "Do you know where my father is?" There was dead silence in the waiting room as we all sat frozen, taken aback, embarrassed and saddened at the petition of such a sweet, innocent young boy. The uniformed deputy bent over with his hands on his knees, smiled, and said, "No, little man, I don't." I could only think, *How sad*; but I had yet to get the revelation as to why I had to witness this heart-wrenching scene. I thought to myself, *He must be here with his teenage mom to visit his father in jail.* Again the sound of the buzz, thump, and slam; and again the little guy runs to the door, "Do you know where my father is?" I thought, *Surely this girl will hold on to him and stop him from this futile quest.* But she did not. That little boy asked six deputies who entered the waiting room the same heartbreaking question, "Do you know where my father is?"

You would have thought his little legs would grow tired running to the door again and again, or that he would grow weary asking the same question and being turned back time and time again. He did not. The deputies patronized him. "I don't know where your father is."

I was there to interview the young man facing prison, but could hardly concentrate on his case. God spoke, "Clyde, that little boy was you." At that precise moment, I was so overwhelmed and assured in my spirit that God had totally mended my broken heart. After interviewing the young man, I could hardly walk to the car or keep my composure; I was so moved by the awesome force of God's presence and deliverance. It occurred to me then how I didn't even want to come and deal with the very atmosphere of jail. Remember, I made a wasted effort to come to the jail *the day before*. How could this moment be so carefully orchestrated to take place a day later? Why couldn't it have been a little girl asking the question, instead of a little boy? This divine moment was a setup by the Father.

If I had found this jail a day earlier, I would have never experienced this miraculous encounter. This was not a coincidence. It was the final healing balm applied to the leaks in *this* vessel. God said, "Clyde, remember how you were always searching and asking, *'God, do you know where my father is? Please send him back home to me.'* And as a little boy, you never grew tired of asking. You would pray and ask me over and over again. I remember Christmas after Christmas; birthday after birthday; and you hoping, praying, and wishing that this is the day my father comes home."

I hadn't come to grips with the truth that those disappointments had twisted into emotional pain because I was disconnected from the father. Without an escort, I grew up in a jail cell in my soul. I would find myself in the waiting room of my heart searching for my root system, thirsty for my strength giver so I could face life. God spoke: *"The prison doors are open; the captives have been set free; leave the waiting room and come to God's table of deliverance."*

These are just some of the struggles I went through without my escort. Like the pro football player alluded to earlier in this chapter, I had experienced success in life. I had college degrees, owned new homes and cars, and operated a very successful business. I attained all these sought-after possessions and accolades; yet, I was living with emotional leaks.

My wife went through years of bewilderment, trying to understand why it was difficult for me to be happy or content. For years, I would not let her into my world. It was not safe for me to trust anyone, fearing they too might leave me. I tried to fix the cracks with educational accomplishments, drugs, and friends, but none of these things could mend my broken heart. In short, I was damaged. I was a leaky vessel, searching for security and stability that was only to be found in God. There is an old gospel song that goes like this, "What can make me whole again? Nothing but the blood of Jesus."

Decades and decades of running to the prison door were finally over. There would be no more buzz, thump, and slam of the door of disappointment for me. It is finished.

Even though I would have successes, I could not accept them because in some way, I believed there was no way I really deserved them since my escort had rejected me.

God has given a new address to all who believe. He calls it the household of faith. As you are nearing the end of this book, I trust you can now say, "My search is over. The question has been answered. I *know* where my father is." God says, "I am right here in your heart. I can never leave you, nor forsake you. Enter into my rest."

I don't know what became of the little guy I saw in the waiting room of the jail that day. I pray for him that he does not go into his adult life without Christ. I pray for his father's release from jail, and that he would acknowledge and accept his God-given assignment to escort his son through life. We don't need another liability in our society. We don't need another athlete, entertainer, politician, or husband who doesn't know God.

One of the fast food restaurants has a meal they call, "The Ultimate," inferring this is as good as it gets. Well, we as believers know we have access to the *ultimate* in fathers. He is as good as it gets. Fathers, learn from him. Tend to your garden and escort your seed, that they might fulfill their destiny without interruption.

Prayer of Deliverance

Abba Father, I pray this prayer of deliverance by faith with confidence in your healing power. You promised in your Word to mend my broken heart, a heart that was broken because of life without the father.

Father, you said in your Word you anointed Jesus to set the captives free. I admit I had been held captive by a childhood that was not escorted and nourished properly.

Father, I now release the pain and discontentment of not receiving love by my earthly father. Heavenly Father, as I'm praying to you, I believe the fears and low self-worth I have experienced are being removed from my soul even as these words are being released from my mouth and received in my ears.

I accept the truth that faith comes by hearing; so I repeat, "I'm free of fears and low self-worth."

My Heavenly Father will never leave me or forsake me. I now forgive my earthly father and hold no unforgiveness towards him. He will never again be a stumbling block for me in expressing love or being loved.

The blood of Jesus has mended all my emotional leaks. All dysfunctional behavior is in my past. I will not return and visit the prison of my childhood, because "whom the Son sets free is free indeed."

I now have an eternal life with the Father.

Bibliography

References:

The Holy Bible, New King James Version® Copyright © 1982 by Thomas Nelson, Inc.

The Holy Bible , New International Version® Copyright © 1978, 1978, 1984 by International Bible Society Published by Zondervan

The Living Bible, Copyright © 1971, Owned by assignment by KNT Charitable Trust Published by Tyndale®

The Message Remix: The Bible in Contemporary Language Copyright © 2003 by Eugene H. Peterson

Ryrie Study Bible , New American Standard Copyright © 1960, 1962, 19963, 1968, 1971, 1972, 1973, 1975, 1977, 1995 By THE LOCKMAN FOUNDATION

Dake's Annotation Reference Bible—The Old and New Testaments, with Notes, Concordance and Index Copyright © 1963, 1991 b6 Finis Jennings Dake

"Nothing But the Blood of Jesus," Curtis Mulder and Robert S. Lowry—Copyright © 2005 Curtis Mulder

CPSIA information
Printed in the USA
LVOW05s1827091

408068LV0

62227